D1458336

Critical Guides to Spanish Texts

Critical Guides to Spanish Texts

EDITED BY J.E. VAREY AND A.D. DEYERMOND

BAROJA

La busca

H. Ramsden

Professor of Spanish Language and Literature
University of Manchester

Grant & Cutler Ltd *in association with*
Tamesis Books Ltd 1982

I.S.B.N. 84-499-5876-8
DEPÓSITO LEGAL: V. 2.078 - 1982

Printed in Spain by
Artes Gráficas Soler, S.A., Valencia
for
GRANT & CUTLER LTD
11 BUCKINGHAM STREET, LONDON, W.C.2

Contents

Prefatory Note

Quotations from *La busca* are according to the first edition published in book form (Madrid: Fernando Fe, 1904) except that obvious printers' errors have been corrected, modern practice has generally been followed in spelling and in the use of accents and abbreviations, and the *Obras completas* punctuation is followed where it seems clearly preferable.Since the 1904 edition is not widely available, page references are to the *Obras completas* (I, 255-373; Madrid: Biblioteca Nueva, 1946), where the text usually but not invariably corresponds. For the sake of readers using other editions I identify extensive key passages also by part and chapter (e.g. III, II). Except where indicated by brackets [...], quotations from the 1903 *El Globo* version of *La busca* follow the newspaper text exactly.

Where possible, all other Baroja quotations and references are based on the Biblioteca Nueva *Obras completas* edition (1946-51). Unfortunately, though the type of this edition has on occasion been reset from one printing to another, with slight changes of pagination, the volumes continue to bear their original date of printing and no declared distinction is therefore possible between successive printings. Because of this, there may be marginal discrepancies between some of my own page references and those applicable to the reader's own copy of the *Obras completas*.

Research for the present study and for a number of associated articles was undertaken with help from the University of Manchester, the British Academy and the Consejo Superior de Investigaciones Científicas.

H.R., 1980

A los amigos de Osán

1. Introduction

During 1961-2 the Spanish literary journal *La Estafeta Literaria* published replies from forty-nine novelists, critics, editors and scholars to their rather ambitious question, '¿Cuáles son las diez mejores novelas del siglo XX?' Since almost all those questioned were Spanish it is presumably not possible to infer from the replies anything relevant to the standing of the Spanish novel in the overall panorama of the twentieth-century novel: at one extreme there were those who listed only Spanish novels; at the other extreme there were those who included no Spanish novel. What is noteworthy, however, is that among Spanish novelists Baroja and Valle-Inclán were those most widely represented and that of all Spanish novels of the twentieth century *La busca* stood out as the most highly esteemed (see editorial comment in No. 242, 1 June 1962). Despite changing tastes and the appearance of a number of outstanding Spanish novels during the last two decades it is probable that a similar survey carried out today would give a basically similar result.

Apart from the intrinsic merits of Baroja's novel-writing, its historical importance, too, is indisputable. Angel María de Lera, a notable novelist of the post-war generation, is one of many to have made the point: 'Aunque sus obras no fuesen tan ricas en valores estéticos y narrativos, bastaría a Baroja el haber renovado en nuestro país el arte de novelar para merecer el puesto que ocupa entre los novelistas españoles del siglo XX, supuesto que ningún otro ha influido tanto como él en el ulterior desarrollo de nuestra literatura novelesca desde los años treinta y, sobre todo, a partir de nuestra guerra civil.' Baroja, he continues, broke with the nineteenth-century concept of the novel as a fully-rounded and self-contained work of art and introduced the 'novela abierta', with the novelist as a detached observer of characters who come and go, almost unrelated to one another, like travellers on a train journey, and whose lives
(. . .)

continue outside and beyond the novel, 'que no termina en un punto, sino en un cruce de caminos, y permite suponer otros muchos desenlaces'. 'Por otra parte', he adds, 'Baroja fue el primer cultivador de las que más tarde se llamarían "novela social" y "novela reportaje", conjuntando en *La busca* ambos elementos de una manera insuperable. *La busca* es, sin duda, nuestra primera gran novela social y nuestra primera gran novela reportaje y, para mí, su obra cumbre' (*12*, pp. 85-6).

But the term 'novela social' opens up an area of much debate: on whether Baroja is concerned primarily with society or with individuals, on whether he approaches society as a critic or simply as an observer and, thence, on the question of his relevance to the socially aware reader of the present day. In this last respect the long accepted view of Baroja as a revolutionary denigrator of established values has been attacked in recent years by a number of younger writers: 'Su espíritu revolucionario, todo lo que hoy llamaría Juan Goytisolo "la destrucción de la España sagrada". No, no hay nada de esto. Es un burgués. No se ha comprometido con nada, no incita a nada revolucionario. Desprecia al pueblo. *No interesa*. Hay, si algo hay que salvar en él, su estilo, su palabra, su lirismo, su música "que durará — dice Sender — lo que dure el castellano"...' (survey by Dámaso Santos, *12*, p. 102).

I shall be concerned inevitably, in the present study, with all these questions: with the question of Baroja's response to society, though without making it the touchstone of my esteem; with the important question of Baroja's break with the nineteenth-century concept of the novel, though without making it the main aim of my study; above all, with the intrinsic characteristics and merits of *La busca* itself, its inimitably Barojan 'valores estéticos y narrativos'.

*   *   *   *   *   *

In a very different primitive version *La busca* first appeared in serial form in the newspaper *El Globo* (fifty-nine instalments; 4 March to 29 May 1903). It comprised an 'Introducción' (subsequently collected in *OC* VIII, 834-8) and six parts. Parts I-III (45,000 words) were revised and published in book form under the title *La lucha por la vida: La busca* (1904; 63,000 words); Parts IV-VI (45,000 words) were revised and published in book form under the title *La lucha por la vida: Mala hierba* (1904; 71,000 words). A third volume, *La lucha por la vida: Aurora roja* (1904), was added to complete the trilogy as we now know it.

A comparison between the two versions throws remarkable light on Baroja as a novelist and I have studied elsewhere the changes made in the transition from *La busca* 1903, Parts I-III, to *La busca* 1904 (*40*). In the present study my main concern is the definitive work. I shall, however, refer also, at times, to the 1903 version to bring out, usually by contrast, certain characteristics of the definitive work.

2. Chronology: 'La busca' in context

Most of Baroja's novels are grouped into series, most commonly trilogies. Of these trilogies *La lucha por la vida* is the most unified, 'sin duda la más unitaria y compacta' (*15*, p. 152; cf. *17*, p. 62; *18*, p. 151), to such an extent that in the opinion of certain commentators the third novel in the trilogy, *Aurora roja*, gives sense and meaning to the other two (*29*, pp. 244-5; *20*, p. 33). For this reason alone it is desirable to glance initially at the whole trilogy and to see *La busca* in context. But there is an even more pressing reason: from the internal evidence of *La busca* alone it is not possible to place the action of the novel precisely in time or, in consequence, to approach the much debated problem of chronology in Baroja. In the outline that follows — schematic for *La busca*, which I assume has been read; slightly fuller for *Mala hierba* and *Aurora roja* — the bracketed years have been arrived at by working back from later evidence, in particular from Manuel's statement near the beginning of *Aurora roja* that he has not seen his brother for fifteen years (p. 525) — that is, since he left Soria at the beginning of *La busca* — and from the most specific historical event depicted in the trilogy, the coronation of Alfonso XIII (17 May 1902; near the end of *Aurora roja*).

La busca

Part I [1885]. Manuel, aged thirteen (or so it appears from subsequent chronology), arrives in Madrid and is allowed to stay with his mother in Doña Casiana's boarding-house — until he comes to blows with one of the guests. His stay at Doña Casiana's seems to extend over a period of about three months, perhaps from May or June to late August or early September.
Part II [1885-6]. Manuel is taken to work and live with his mother's cousin, Ignacio, down in the poor quarter of Madrid. For the boy as for the reader it offers another range of

experiences. By piecing together Baroja's main chronological indications ('Una mañana de fines de septiembre', p. 290; 'A los dos o tres meses de estancia en el Corralón', p. 295; 'Unos meses después', p. 303; 'Una noche de agosto', p. 310; 'Era ya a principios de otoño', p. 319; 'Un par de semanas después', p. 322) we find that Leandro's death, with which Part II closes, occurs somewhat more than a year after Manuel's move to the poor quarter.

Part III [1886-8]. Ignacio falls ill and 'al cabo de dos o tres semanas' (p. 324) Manuel has to leave. His mother places him first in a greengrocer's and breadshop, then 'a los tres meses de entrar allá' (p. 326) in a bakery. 'Durante dos meses que pasó Manuel en la tahona, vivió como un autómata' (p. 329). When he falls ill he returns to Doña Casiana's but is ejected after a few weeks when he is found in compromising circumstances with Doña Casiana's niece, much developed during the last two years and now 'hecha una mujer' (p. 329). He wanders out to the slum area, returns briefly to Doña Casiana's during Lent [1887] to be with his mother as she dies, drifts out to the slums again and spends the summer with Vidal and El Bizco. A house-breaking fiasco in August is followed by 'un par de meses' (p. 354) of involvement with prostitutes, after which Vidal goes off with a flower-girl and Manuel is turned out for non-payment of rent. 'A principios de noviembre' (p. 354) Manuel is picked up by Señor Custodio and spends the next twelve months living with him and his wife — until the following November when he comes to blows with Justa's suitor, resolves not to return to Custodio's and finishes up in the Puerta del Sol, huddled together with other vagrants.

Mala hierba

The chronology of the transition from *La busca* to *Mala hierba* is unclear. Since *La busca* ends with Manuel's resolution to work and *Mala hierba* begins in the same vein, one could reasonably infer that the one follows on directly from the other and find support for this in Manuel's own statement at the beginning of *Mala hierba* that he has been without work 'desde hace unos días' (p. 379). On the other hand, Manuel's good intentions recur fairly frequently and are therefore no guarantee of chronological continuity; it is possible to assume unnarrated adventures between one volume and the next, especially since Manuel is now resolved on a '*cambio* de vida' (p. 377; my italics), as though he had been odd-jobbing and *golfeando* again since his exemplary twelve months with Custodio. What is certain is that the first clearly placed event in *Mala hierba* is in early November, at least two months, more probably three to four months and (if one wishes to assume a direct transition from *La busca*) not impossibly twelve months after the opening of the novel. It cannot, then, be the same November in which *La busca* ended and I assume it to be the following November [1889]. It could conceivably, though not probably, be a later year.

Part I [1888/9(?)-90]. Manuel searches out Roberto and is allowed to stay in the studio that Roberto shares with Alex, a bohemian sculptor of limited talents. He is subsequently taken over by another bohemian, Santín, a lay-about who wants help in setting up a photographic studio, but Santín gets married in early November and dismisses Manuel a fortnight later. For the next eleven months more or less — November [1889] to October [1890] — Manuel, now eighteen (p. 395), is passed off with false documentation as the son of the Baronesa de Aynant — a means of extorting money from a former lover of the Baronesa, the alleged father of Manuel. When the ruse is discovered and finances dry up, the Baronesa and her daughter go off to live with a brother-in-law in Belgium, leaving Manuel behind.

Part II [1890-2]. Roberto finds Manuel a job as an apprentice compositor. 'Para la primavera [1891], Manuel componía con facilidad' (p. 432) and, at about that time, he goes to live with one of his workmates, Jesús, in the Ronda de Toledo. On Christmas Eve three men come to study the poverty and needs of the area, and Jesús' sister, La Fea, takes in an orphaned girl and her baby brother. The girl, Salvadora, sets about organizing the household, but Jesús chafes at so much organization and goes off on a spree with Manuel. By the time they return to the

printing-shop two days later they have been sacked. They spend
the next weeks and months (March-May [1892]) living rough and
begging, with no attempt to find work, and in May they are
caught sleeping in the Church of San Sebastián and handed over
to the police. Manuel alleges a connection with the press and is
promptly released. As he huddles under the arcades of the Plaza
Mayor he is joined by a veteran of the Cuban war and together
they steal valuables from a man who has just committed suicide
and then hunt out another Cuban war veteran, Marcos
Calatrava, El Cojo, for help with the disposal of the goods.
Calatrava's secretary turns out to be Vidal and Manuel is given a
room in Vidal's lodgings.

Part III [1892-3]. Manuel is taken on by Calatrava and becomes
involved in gaming frauds, again meets Custodio's daughter
Justa, now turned prostitute, and goes to live with her. There is
a time-leap from winter [1892-3] to the following August when
Manuel, Vidal and their prostitute companions go to see a public
execution. On the following day, during a picnic in which they
are joined by Calatrava and his woman, Vidal is stabbed to
death, apparently by El Bizco. Manuel and the others slip away
but Manuel is finally traced by the police and taken in for
questioning. His age, apparently in September, is said to be
twenty-one (p. 492). If one assumes his birthday to be in
October, this is not incompatible with the statement, in
November four years earlier, that he was then eighteen (p.
395).When he proceeds to reveal the frauds in which he has been
involved, influence is exerted from above to effect his release —
on condition that he will help the police to find El Bizco. He
collaborates, without success, for two days but is released
unconditionally when he threatens to denounce the fraud
conspiracy completely if he is not left alone.

Aurora roja

Prologue [?]. Juan, a young seminarist on holiday at home,
decides not to return to the seminary for the new session and sets
out to walk to Barcelona.

Part I [1900]. One April, years later, that former seminarist searches out his brother Manuel in Madrid and settles there. They have not seen each other for fifteen years (p. 525). In the meantime, Juan has entered and left the seminary, been a travelling player, studied and practised art in Barcelona and established himself as a sculptor in Paris. Since the end of *Mala hierba*, Manuel, after a year of lapses under Jesús' influence, has gradually become more ordered in his ways and now lives in the north of Madrid with a widowed sister and with Salvadora and her young brother. During the next couple of months Manuel meets several reminders of his past life and is helped by Roberto and, despite certain anarchist misgivings about bourgeois ownership, by Juan to set himself up with his own printing-press.

Part II [1900-1]. A nearby bar, La Aurora, becomes a Sunday meeting-place for Juan and his anarchist associates. In November Manuel goes to a number of meetings and hears different forms of anarchism advocated, and the following February Roberto visits him in his printing-shop and discourses on Spanish society. Manuel takes on a manager, Pepe Morales, and attends further anarchist meetings. The police investigate thefts from a nearby cemetery and Manuel learns that El Bizco has now been arrested and will probably be sentenced to death. Don Alonso's involvement in the arrest prompts a flashback chapter on his life during the last few years and El Bizco's death sentence prompts a visit by Manuel both to him and to the public executioner.

Part III [1901-2]. Juan falls ill and is moved to Manuel's house, with subsequent debates between Juan the anarchist and Morales the socialist. Manuel finds something crazy about all the anarchists but as Juan's illness becomes more serious he is brought more closely into contact with them and in January [1902] he attends a meeting in the Barbieri Theatre and is present at a private meeting to discuss the possibility of setting up a radical newspaper. As the date of the Coronation approaches, an anarchist contact of Juan's stays in Manuel's house and is found to have with him a bomb which is disposed of on Salvadora's initiative. Roberto calls and holds forth at length to

Manuel on society and its evils, on democracy and aristocracy, on the need to stimulate will, etc. He also makes a present to Manuel of the printing-shop that he has principally financed and urges him to marry Salvadora. Manuel marries, the Coronation passes off without notable incident and Juan is brought home gravely ill. He dies as the police come to arrest him and is buried on the following day.

*   *   *   *   *   *

Even from this brief outline we can glimpse some of the more notable features of Baroja's writing. In particular we can see that the narration is linear and episodic: a simple linear progression sustained by the presence of Manuel is filled out with a succession of scenes, characters and events; in Manuel's company we advance from one point to another, stop and look around, move on, stop and look around again, and so forth. Moreover, there is little attention to any progression of events or character development or causal relationship during the move forward (a point that is nicely confirmed by the apparent ease with which Baroja added and shifted characters, scenes and events in the 1903-4 revision, *40*). Instead, Baroja offers simply a brief pointer to the time elapsed ('Después de callejear toda la mañana', 'Al cabo de dos o tres semanas', 'Unos meses después') or an indication of the new point in time ('Por la tarde', 'Una mañana de fines de septiembre', 'Era ya a principios de otoño'). What is important for him, it seems, is not time's passing but Manuel's successive standpoints in time and what can be observed from them.

And what we most frequently observe in this trilogy are degrading scenes and degraded people: sordidness, poverty, low life, immorality, insensitivity, bitterness, violence.... But there are also exotic and eccentric characters and some of them have been mentioned in the above outline: the student Roberto, part English, part Spanish; Don Alonso, the former circus manager; Alex and his bohemian associates; the Baronesa de Aynant, a Cuban adventuress, widow of a Belgian aristocrat.... Moreover, in *Aurora roja* we are present also at innumerable discourses and debates on Spanish society and its ills, with different views on if and how those ills can be remedied, and the presence of these discourses and debates gives strength to views of *Aurora roja* as the logical outcome and climax of the whole trilogy: after the long succession of degrading scenes, the debate on a possible solution. It is a tempting hypothesis and there is support for it in the 1903-4 revision. Nevertheless, it seems that this was not the author's original intention. Apart from the absence of *Aurora roja* from the 1903 version, evidence in the 1904 version itself suggests that in the early stages of composition — and even at a fairly advanced stage — Baroja had no thought of adding *Aurora roja*. *Aurora roja*, it seems, was an afterthought, even a late afterthought. I shall approach the question not by external chronology of writing, but by internal chronology of the trilogy itself.

As a starting-point one has to note a number of anachronisms. Except for the first, which is much referred to by critics, I confine myself to evidence from *La busca*:

1. In *Mala hierba* (pp. 463-4) a veteran of the Cuban campaign recalls Weyler's 'guerra de exterminio' (1896) and the subsequent loss of the island (1898). Since he has spent at least one winter in Spain since his return from Cuba (p. 463) he cannot be speaking earlier than 1899. However, from internal chronology as outlined above he is in fact speaking in 1892.

2. I went to Paris in 1868, says Don Alonso (p. 306), and four months later [i.e. 1868 or 1869] I went to America and 'dos o tres años después' [i.e. at some time during 1870-2] I knew Rosita who would then be twenty-five or thirty [i.e. she was born during the period 1840-7]. 'De manera que la Rosita que usted dice tendría ahora sesenta y tantos — dijo Roberto', in which case Roberto, hardly the sort of person to make an error of calculation in such a matter, is speaking not earlier than 1901. According to internal chronology, however, he is speaking in 1886.

3. In 1883 (internal chronology) Manuel was sent to stay with his uncle, 'jefe de un apeadero' in the province of Soria, and in 1885, to get from there to Madrid, he took a train first to

Almazán, then to Alcuneza, then to Madrid (pp. 263-4). But in 1883, as in 1885, no railway line existed in the province of Soria. The one referred to by Baroja was the first to be opened: in the summer of 1892.[1] There is an anachronism, then, by at least nine years.

4. The phonograph was invented, named and demonstrated by Edison in 1877-8, abandoned for a number of years, taken up and developed by Bell and Tainter in the mid 1880s and produced commercially from 1887. However, because of its high price it became established in Europe only gradually during the 1890s when the Pathé brothers developed phonograph manufacture and recording, notably from 1894.[2] Don Alonso's 1886 'fonógrafo' (pp. 305-6), then, is an anachronism. So also, though by a smaller gap, is his 1886 'Torre *Infiel*' ('Torre Eiffel' in the 1903 version), for the Eiffel Tower was not built until 1887-9.

5. In the 1886 story of his pursuit by a giant crab Don Alonso compares its 'fa... fa... fa...' to that of an 'automóvil' (p. 321). In fact, car production hardly developed before 1897 and the first cars appeared in Spain at some time between 1897 and 1900.[3] Consequently, Don Alonso's 1886 reference is another notable anachronism, especially since it assumes understanding by the inhabitants of the Corralón.

6. The music-box in Doña Casiana's boarding-house [in 1885] plays 'el "Gentil pastor" de *La mascota* y el vals de *La diva*' (p. 271) and the band at the *kermesse* [in 1886] plays 'el schotis de *Los cocineros*' and 'el pasodoble de *El tambor de granaderos*' (pp. 311-12). *La mascota* was first produced in 1880,

---

[1] Francisco Wais, *Historia de los ferrocarriles españoles*, 2nd ed. (Madrid, 1974), pp. 431-2, 723.

[2] *Encyclopaedia Britannica*, XVII (1969), 901-3 ('Phonograph').

[3] *Enciclopedia Espasa-Calpe*, VI [1909], 1176; *Gaceta de Madrid*, 13 August 1897 (a *Real Orden* laying down general criteria for self-propelled vehicles in response to an application for permission to use a steam-driven vehicle); first car registered in Spain on 31 October 1900 (*Anuario Automovilista de España: Año 1965-66*, Barcelona, pp. 10-D, 14-D); first noted use of the word 'automóvil' in a Government *Reglamento* dated 20 March 1900.

La diva (in its Spanish adaptation) in 1885, *Los cocineros* in 1897 and *El tambor de granaderos* in 1894.[4] The last two, then, are clearly anachronisms.

7. El Expósito [in 1887] tells Manuel of the food given out at the María Cristina barracks, near Atocha station, and takes him along there (pp. 335-6). But the María Cristina barracks were not completed and given their name until some time between 1892 and 1895.[5]

8. El Expósito also tells Manuel that in winter he sleeps in 'las calderas de asfalto' (p. 335), and near the end of *La busca* [1888] we see those 'calderas' and are told: 'Estaban asfaltando un trozo de la Puerta del Sol' (p. 370). In fact, asphalting in Madrid did not start until 1900: first, the Puerta del Sol (1900), then 'las calles más importantes' (1901).[6]

9. Señor Custodio's dog, Reverte (p. 358 [1887]), is presumably named after the bullfighter Antonio Reverte, 'torero de leyenda', 'uno de los toreros más traídos y llevados en las coplas y en los romances'.[7] But in 1887 Antonio Reverte was only seventeen. He did not commence his bullfighting career until 1890 and he took the *alternativa* only in 1891.

10. 'Nos han derribado las cuevas de la Montaña — dijo el Bizco' (p. 370 [1888]). If these are the same as 'las cuevas de la Moncloa', as I believe they are, they still existed at the beginning of 1902 (*El Globo*, 2 February 1902), but were presumably destroyed shortly afterwards in the vigorous transformation of that area of Madrid undertaken by order of the Governor ('En

---

[4] I am indebted to Maribel López Pérez for research in the music archive of the Sociedad General de Autores in Madrid.

[5] The Cuartel de María Cristina is included in the list of barracks in the 1896 *Almanaque y guía matritense* (Madrid [1895]), p. 78, but not in the 1893 edition (Madrid, 1892), p. 54. Documents in the Madrid Municipal Archive suggest that work on and around the barracks was still in progress in 1894 (10—111—1 and 35).

[6] F.C. Sainz de Robles, *Historias y estampas de la villa de Madrid*, Madrid, II [1934], 714. See also Baroja's own article on the asphalting of the Puerta del Sol: 'Humo' (*El País*, 17 September 1900; not in *OC*).

[7] Federico Bravo Morata, *Fin del siglo y de las colonias* (Madrid, 1972), p. 103.

1901 Alberto Aguilera mandó transformar los desmontes del NO, en el bellísimo Parque del Oeste').[8]

This survey does not pretend to be exhaustive. There are other cases that I have lacked time to pursue (for example, the date of the first appearance on the bullfighting scene of Don Tancredo, a famous *espontáneo* of the beginning of the twentieth century who can hardly have been active as early as 1885, p. 297);[9] there are also, presumably, others that I have overlooked. However, the examples listed suffice for our present purpose.

They oblige us, of course, to look critically at the chronological outline proposed above. They also encourage us to look sympathetically at chronological interpretations different from my own in the hope that they will resolve the anachronisms. Unfortunately none of those so far published is helpful in this respect:

    1. Blanco Aguinaga says simply that the action of the trilogy takes place 'Aproximadamente entre 1890 y 1902' but does not seek to justify his claim (*29*, p. 243).

    2. Puértolas, working back from the Coronation and from Manuel's statement at the beginning of *Aurora roja* that he and his brother have not seen each other for fifteen years, calculates, as I do, that the trilogy covers the years 1885-1902 but, for no declared reason, assumes a gap of four years between *La busca* and *Mala hierba*, with a corresponding reduction of the gap between *Mala hierba* and *Aurora roja* (*20*, pp. 11-12). Since the only two indications of Manuel's age appear in *Mala hierba* this reduces Manuel's age in *La busca* by four years and Puértolas says that he is ten when the trilogy opens, an inappropriate age, I suggest, for some of Manuel's actions and reactions. Besides, the absence of flashback survey at the beginning of *Mala hierba* — except for a brief reference to contact with his sister, which might explain a few months — does not suggest that much time has elapsed since the end of *La busca* (contrast the extensive flashback surveys at the beginning of *Aurora roja*). Finally, the

[8] Sainz de Robles, *Historias y estampas*, II, 714.

[9] Federico Bravo Morata, *El sainete madrileño y la España de sainete* (Madrid, 1973), p. 72.

evidence of *La busca* 1903, with the additional information that Manuel 'tenía ya quince años' when he was moved from the 'puesto de pan' to the bakery (*El Globo*, 22 March 1903), points clearly to continuity between *La busca* and *Mala hierba*.

3. Beltrán de Heredia, concerned about the anachronism of the Cuban veteran, rejects Puértolas' dependence on 'la vaga referencia a los quince años que Manuel dice haber estado separado de su hermano', equates the 'crimen de la calle de Malasaña' (*LB* I,IV) with the real-life crime of the Calle de Fuencarral (1888), and thus places the beginning of the novel in 1888; thereafter, accepting Puértolas' doubtful notion of a four-year gap between *La busca* and *Mala hierba*, he goes on to argue that 'el repatriado aparecerá, justamente, en 1898' (*24*, pp. 150-1). This, however, does not solve the anachronism of the 'repatriado' who, as we have seen, has spent at least one winter back in Spain since the loss of the island and cannot therefore be speaking earlier than 1899. Besides, Manuel's reference to the fifteen years since he last saw his brother is in no way 'vague'. Finally, it is extremely doubtful whether a real-life crime in which all the relevant names have been changed can be adduced as firm evidence of chronological placing (see below, p. 27, n. 10).

4. Alarcos Llorach, in a closer scrutiny of the text, opposes Puértolas' (and thence also Beltrán de Heredia's) notion of a four-year gap between *La busca* and *Mala hierba* ('así sus [Manuel's] vicisitudes van más de acuerdo con la edad'), notes that Manuel tells Roberto at the beginning of *Mala hierba* that he has been without work 'desde hace unos días' and infers from this that *Mala hierba* follows on immediately after the end of *La busca*, thus assuming that Manuel spends a whole year with Alex and his bohemian associates. More doubtfully, he follows Beltrán de Heredia in accepting the Calle de Fuencarral crime as a more reliable chronological indication of when the novel begins than Manuel's specific statement ('La separación de Juan y Manuel, que se dice ser de quince años, es en realidad de doce'). Lastly, he points to an alleged 'evidente inconsecuencia' between the two indications of Manuel's age, thus overlooking

the possibility that the author, albeit with a chronological precision unusual in his writings, had mentally placed Manuel's birthday in October (*36*, pp. 52-5).

We can return now to the ten headings under which I earlier indicated anachronisms. The first, that of the 'repatriado de Cuba' and his story, is the one most commonly referred to by scholars and it remains an anachronism whichever of the above chronological interpretations one accepts: by at least one year if one accepts Beltrán de Heredia's arguments, by at least four years if one accepts the outline proposed by Puértolas or the different one proposed by Alarcos Llorach, and by at least seven years if one accepts my own interpretation. The second anachronism indicated, that of Rosita's age, has been noted, I believe, only by Alarcos Llorach, who left it unresolved (*36*, pp. 55-6). To the best of my knowledge none of the other eight examples of anachronism has previously been pointed out and none of them is resolved whichever of the above chronological interpretations one accepts. In view of this, there seems little point in exerting oneself, against Manuel's clear statement of a fifteen-year gap since he last saw his brother, to place the beginning of the novel in 1888 rather than 1885. It would solve the anachronism of the Eiffel Tower, which I indicated only in passing and not as one of my main ten points, and give the Calle de Fuencarral crime a chronological authority that it does not deserve, but nothing else. As one reads *La busca* in the overall context of the trilogy one simply has to accept that there are anachronisms and to bear them in mind when considering the much emphasized documentary value of the novel.

Having established that there are anachronisms we must seek to explain them. One may, of course, simply argue that Baroja was evolving a more open, freer, less fettered type of novel, and Alarcos Llorach, in this respect, has emphasized the difference between 'tiempo *histórico*' and 'tiempo *novelístico*' and gone on to compare 'el tiempo narrativo con el tiempo real transcurrido' (*36*, pp. 56 ff.). *La busca* 1903, which Alarcos Llorach apparently did not know, seems to offer a better explanation. Its action, we have seen, corresponds to that of *La busca* 1904 plus

Mala hierba 1904 and it takes place over a period of seven years (increased to eight in the 1904 revision). In the absence of *Aurora roja*, with the Coronation and with Manuel's reference to a fifteen-year absence from his brother, we are not tied to the years 1885-93 and in fact *La busca* 1903 most probably covers the years 1895-1902 (*40*). Given this time range the majority of the anachronisms indicated earlier are immediately resolved: Manuel no longer catches the train from Soria before the line existed, no longer hears music from zarzuelas before those zarzuelas were written, no longer queues for food at a barracks before the building of the barracks was even started... and the Cuban veteran's story is placed not in 1892 but in 1901. In the definitive version of the trilogy these events became anachronisms because of the addition of *Aurora roja* and the consequent pushing back in time of the action of *La busca* 1903.

Consequently, whatever sense *Aurora roja* may give to the definitive trilogy, it seems that Baroja did not have *Aurora roja* in mind when he wrote *La busca* 1903 and that Blanco Aguinaga is therefore mistaken when, in line with other scholars, he describes the trilogy as 'un proyecto bien estructurado y perfectamente llevado a cabo en un solo tirón de dos años de trabajo' (*29*, p. 245). Nor can one easily accept that Alarcos Llorach's sophisticated distinction between 'tiempo *histórico*' and 'tiempo *novelístico*' is either necessary or justified, or that there is any novelistic advantage in the anachronism of the 'repatriado' and his Cuban reminiscences, especially in a writer who prided himself on the documentary value of his novels. As a study of the 1903 revision clearly shows, Baroja struggled hard with the chronological problems caused by the addition of *Aurora roja* and changed several passages where there would otherwise have been a glaring anachronism in the revised version. But the Cuban veteran's reminiscences could less easily be moved — or removed —, for the 'repatriado' was Manuel's means of introduction to Calatrava, another veteran of the Cuban campaign, and thence to a substantial series of experiences, and much rewriting and much loss of vivid material would have been caused by submission to real-life chronology. Baroja, then, ever reluctant to lose vivid material (*40*), was prepared to disregard the resulting anachronization of the 'repatriado' and his reminiscences. He presumably overlooked the other anachronisms referred to above. Since his commentators have done likewise, this is perhaps understandable. The anachronisms are, nevertheless, still weaknesses. The reader should be on his guard against attempts to find evidence of advanced narrative techniques where there is perhaps only neglect or oversight on the part of the author.

The 1903-4 revision, with the pushing back in time of the action of *La busca* 1903 from 1895-1902 to 1885-93, does not explain all the anachronisms indicated earlier. Several were already anachronisms in *La busca* 1903 (most notably the reference to the 'automóvil' and to the Cuevas de la Montaña and the 'calderas de asfalto') and one anachronism was added in the 1903-4 revision (Don Alonso's chronological references to Rosita which were absent from *La busca* 1903). We are touching here on another notable feature of Baroja's writing: his tendency to describe always 'por impresión directa' (VII, 1053), from his own present observation post, and thereafter to project these 'apuntes del natural' into the past of his novel, at times with disregard of the resulting anachronism. Thus, in an article published in *El País* (17 September 1900; not in *OC*) Baroja described the asphalting of the Puerta del Sol that was currently in progress. He clearly drew on this experience when he came to write *La busca* 1903 but placed the asphalting in 1898, when the Puerta del Sol in fact still had only its sets ('adoquines'). The 1903-4 revision forced the asphalting even further back, to 1888. Don Alonso's references to Rosita offer an even clearer example. His standpoint as he talks cannot be earlier than 1901. Internal chronology, however, obliges us to place it in 1886. The explanation seems evident: Baroja wrote Don Alonso's story from his own standpoint in time (perhaps 1903) and neglected to make the necessary change in calculation in order to integrate the story into the chronological context of the novel. Similarly, in *Mala hierba* (pp. 484-5 [winter of 1892-3]) Baroja refers to the inauguration of the Salón París and the debut of the Coronela's

daughter La Chuchita. As Alarcos Llorach has noted (*36*, p. 50),
Baroja subsequently identified this character with the real-life
Chelito (VII, 754-5) at whose debut the author was present in
1900. Yet again, then, Baroja's own observational standpoint
close to the moment of writing has been projected into the past
of the novel. Similarly again, to take an example finally from
outside the trilogy, Baroja himself has pointed out that in *El
escuadrón del brigante*, the second volume of his *Memorias de
un hombre de acción*, 'los guerrilleros [de 1809] son tipos vistos
en los pueblos de la provincia de Burgos el año 1914' (VII,
1075).[10] What matters in Baroja, it seems, are the author's own
experiences and observations which he thereupon places,
somewhat haphazardly, at various chronological points in his
novels. Manuel's journey through time is Baroja's journey
through the Spain of his day. Chronology is forced on Baroja by
the form of his novel, but he is not a historical novelist. His
vision is basically present: responses to the world in which he
himself was immersed.

This may seem a strange suggestion to make about the author
of the twenty-two volumes of *Memorias de un hombre de acción*
as well as of other books inspired in Spain's past. However, it is

[10] Even here there is a slight but nicely revealing error of chronology: *El
escuadrón del brigante* was published in 1913; Baroja could hardly have seen
his 'guerrilleros' in 1914. On the same Barojan characteristic noted above,
see also the eye-witness evidence of the author's nephew on the later period of
his writings: 'De acuerdo con esta técnica de transferir al pasado compuso
también novelas enteras, como *Las mascaradas sangrientas* (1927), en el que
un crimen que hubo en Guipúzcoa, el llamado "crimen de Beizama", lo
aprovechó colocando su desenvolvimiento en la primera guerra carlista (Julio
Caro Baroja, *Los Baroja*, Madrid, 1972, p. 80) — a further indication,
incidentally, that the Fuencarral crime is an unreliable basis for chronological
dating. In his study of *El mundo es ansí*, Critical Guides to Spanish Texts, 20
(London, 1977), pp. 62-3, C.A. Longhurst has sought to defend Baroja
against accusations of slipshod chronology. However, the evidence of *El
mundo es ansí* itself shows this defence to be ill-founded. If one constructs
the chronology of the novel from the declared fact that Sacha first left Russia
for Geneva in the wake of the workers' rising in Moscow (December 1905)
one sees that the narrator can hardly have been given Sacha's papers until
some time after 1916. Since the novel was first published in 1912 this is
manifestly impossible.

worth noting Baroja's own declaration in 1920, when he had already published ten volumes of the *Memorias*: 'Desde hace algún tiempo me he metido en el campo de la novela histórica, pero no estoy completamente a mi gusto en él y tengo que salir para hacer mis escaraceos y ocuparme de las cosas del día' (V, 229). In fact, in his historical novels too he concerns himself with 'las cosas del día'. 'Tal vez no haya ninguna novela de Baroja', comments Maravall, 'que se pueda calificar plenamente de novela histórica'; in the *Memorias de un hombre de acción* 'no se trata de buscar datos arqueológicos, eruditos, cuya suma en más de veinte volúmenes es bien reducida, sino de captar de verdad materiales humanos, a través de los cuales alcanzar la experiencia directa y personal del humano viviente' (*10*, Ī, pp. 166, 170).

This finding is relevant not only to Baroja. It is relevant also to the 1898 Generation in general, for, despite the much proclaimed historicism of the Generation, there is little awareness of history in any modern sense. History, for the principal members of the Generation — including its historians — was not a chronologically evolving complex of social, economic and political structures. It was a biological organism with an unchanging backbone of 'eternal values' that could best be discovered through personal contact with the living present. But personal contact and individual response are difficult to separate and the writers of '98 did not attempt to separate them. Ultimately, for each of them, Spain past and present became a projection outwards of individual responses to specifically observed present realities. Baroja's own vision, I repeat, is basically present: responses to the world in which he himself was immersed.

3. Representative pages

In the previous chapter, apart from the emphasis on chronology, the brief outline of the trilogy helped us also to glimpse some of the most striking characteristics of Baroja's writing, notably the rope and knots construction and the emphasis on human degradation. In the present chapter a study of representative pages will serve to throw further light on these characteristics. The pages to be examined are from *La busca*, Part II, Chapter I. Manuel has been expelled from Doña Casiana's boarding-house and been delivered by his mother to her cousin's cobbler's shop. He has met various members of the family, spent his first nights there with the grandmother and, on the following Sunday, been collected by his cousin Vidal and taken home for lunch. We join the story at the moment of their arrival:

> Pasaron adentro; era la casa del señor Ignacio pequeña: la componían dos alcobas, una sala, la cocina y un cuarto oscuro. El primer cuarto era la sala, amueblada con una cómoda de pino, un sofá, varias sillas de paja y un espejo verde, lleno de cromos y de fotografías, envuelto en una gasa roja. Solía la familia del zapatero hacer de comedor este cuarto los domingos, por ser el más espacioso y el de más luz. (p. 282)

There are three main elements: progression via the initial preterite to carry Manuel and his cousin — and the reader — into Ignacio's house ('Pasaron adentro'), description via a series of imperfects to evoke the scene within ('era la casa...') — in miniature, the rope and knots construction that we observed in the overall progression of the trilogy —, and generalization, as the author intervenes to place the immediate experience in a wider context ('Solía la familia...'). The third of these elements was added in 1904 and we shall see the significance of this later.

The same three elements are present also in the next paragraph:

Cuando llegaron Manuel y Vidal hacía tiempo que los esperaban. Sentáronse todos a la mesa, y la Salomé, la cuñada del zapatero, se encargó de servir la comida. Manuel no conocía a la Salomé. Era parecidísima a su hermana, la madre de Vidal. Las dos, de mediana estatura, tenían la nariz corta y descarada, los ojos negros y hermosos; a pesar de su semejanza física, las diferenciaba por completo su aspecto: la madre de Vidal, llamada Leandra, sucia, despeinada, astrosa, con trazas de mal humor, parecía mucho más vieja que la Salomé, aunque no la llevaba más que tres o cuatro años. La Salomé mostraba en su semblante un aire alegre y decidido.

Preterites to carry the action forward, imperfects to describe what is seen (with the words 'Manuel no conocía a la Salomé' to remind us that our viewpoint is close to Manuel's) and authorial intervention to open up perspectives ('hacía tiempo que los esperaban') or to point out when appearances belie reality ('Leandra...parecía mucho más vieja que la Salomé, aunque no la llevaba más que tres o cuatro años'). These examples of authorial intervention, too, were added in 1904. There is a further significant difference between the 1903 and 1904 versions and I quote the final lines of the 1903 version to facilitate comparison:

lo que las diferenciaba por completo era que la zapatera estaba sucia, despeinada, astrosa, con expresión de mal humor, y la Salomé vestía bien, iba peinada a lo Mazzantini y tenía una expresión simpática.

In the 1903 version the description of the attractive Salomé is as full as that of her sister; in the 1904 version the emphasis is clearly on the repulsive Leandra. This observation brings us close to the second notable feature of Baroja's style noted in the trilogy outline: the emphasis on human degradation.

The evidence so far is slight but justifies an initial hypothesis that I shall go on to confirm: in 1904 Baroja takes greater advantage of his right to authorial intervention and omniscience; along with this more clearly assumed right he guides his reader more than he did in 1903, especially towards a more sombre view of reality, with the playing down of attractive elements and greater emphasis on unattractive elements. With this in mind we can pass on to the following paragraph which offers ample illustration of these points:

> ¡Y lo que es la suerte! La Leandra, a pesar de su abandono, de su humor agrio y de su afición al aguardiente, estaba casada con un hombre trabajador y bueno, y, en cambio, la Salomé, dotada de excelentes condiciones de laboriosidad y buen genio, había concluido amontonándose con un gachó entre estafador, descuidero y matón, del cual tenía dos hijos. Por un espíritu de humildad o de esclavitud, unido a un natural independiente y bravío, la Salomé adoraba a su hombre y se engañaba a sí misma para considerarlo como tremendo y bragado, aunque era un cobarde y un gandul. El bellaco se había dado cuenta clara de la cosa, y cuando le parecía bien, con un ceño terrible aparecía en la casa y exigía los cuartos que la Salomé ganaba cosiendo a máquina, a cinco céntimos las dos varas. Ella le daba sin pena el producto de su penoso trabajo, y muchas veces el truhán no se contentaba con sacarle el dinero, sino que la zurraba además. (p. 283)[11]

After the rather Galdosian exclamation at the beginning (an example of authorial intervention that was already present in 1903) one observes that the words 'Manuel pudo enterarse después que' (1903) have been deleted from *La busca* 1904 so that the whole of what follows is presented, in 1904, not as a subsequent discovery by Manuel but on the authority of the narrator himself. Moreover, in 1904 Baroja takes advantage of his now omniscient standpoint to guide his reader's reaction

---

[11] Compare the corresponding 1903 version:

> ¡Y lo que es la suerte! Manuel pudo enterarse después que la Felisa, sucia, chismosa y aficionada al aguardiente, se había casado con un hombre como el zapatero, honrado y trabajador, y en cambio la Salomé, con todas sus excelentes condiciones de mujer trabajadora y buena, se había amontonado con un *gachó* medio estafador, medio descuidero, del cual tenía dos hijos y á quien no veía más que cuando iba á sacarle los cuartos que ella ganaba trabajando como una negra, cosiendo á máquina á cinco céntimos las dos varas. Y muchas veces no se contentaba con sacarle el dinero, sino que la zurraba además. (*El Globo*, 11 March 1903)

more closely than he did in 1903. Thus, in the description of Salomé and her husband there is far greater emphasis in 1904 on the husband's bestial nature (with the addition of such response-guiding words as 'matón', 'cobarde', 'gandul', 'bellaco' and 'truhán') — some ten lines in all, in contrast to the briefly dismissed Ignacio, 'un hombre trabajador y bueno' —, greater attention to Salomé's inexplicable admiration for this brute of a man (with the author's added indication that she was misguided in her admiration), and greater emphasis on her submissiveness, with the added words, 'Ella le daba sin pena el producto de su penoso trabajo', which serve both to arouse our sympathy for her and to emphasize further her husband's brutality.

Such changes are characteristic of the 1903-4 revision and they oblige us to reject outright the endlessly repeated suggestion that Baroja was an objective writer. His treatment was scarcely objective in *La busca* 1903; in *La busca* 1904 it became far less objective. Whereas in 1903 Baroja stood more obviously outside his narration, in *La busca* 1904 he becomes personally involved, sympathizing occasionally, condemning frequently and adding whole paragraphs in which he himself, as the omniscient narrator, places specific here-and-now observations in a wider context, with frequent — and peculiarly Barojan — comments on the significance of what is observed. There is ample further evidence of all these things in my comparative study of the two versions (*40*).

As we move forward in time we are reminded again of Manuel:

> En la comida, Manuel escuchó sin terciar en la conversación. Se habló de una de las muchachas de la vecindad que se había ido con un chalán muy rico, hombre casado y con familia.
>
> —Ha hecho bien —dijo la Leandra, vaciando un vaso de vino [etc.; 35 more lines].

The words 'Manuel escuchó sin terciar en la conversación' are especially significant: Manuel is both the link between successive episodes and our guide to what is observed, but he himself takes little or no part in the action described; here as elsewhere the emphasis is on the world around him. But in the conversation that follows, Baroja omits the trivialities and platitudes of family table-talk and concentrates on a single topic which he introduces in a few words, apparently condensed from conversation that is not included. Thereafter, the emphasis is on Leandra's immoral views and coarse expression, with character insights and comments that suggest the narrator rather than a thirteen-year-old boy: 'la Salomé, que quería discutir la cuestión impersonalmente' (absent in 1903); 'El señor Ignacio se sentía ofendido y desvió la conversación'. Significantly, what Leandra says is not related to her subsequent role in the novel, for she scarcely appears again. Nor does it serve as an influence on Manuel's own later actions. Here as elsewhere in the novel, manifestations of bestial behaviour are valid in their own right. They seem both to fascinate Baroja and to disgust him, and lest we ourselves fail to share his disgust, the reactions of Ignacio the husband and Leandro the son are there to guide us: 'El señor Ignacio desvió con disgusto la vista de su mujer, y el hijo mayor, Leandro, miró a su madre de un modo torvo y severo.' After a reference to the 'crimen de las Peñuelas', the meal is over — after perhaps two minutes of actual conversation — and with a momentary reference to Manuel, our observation point, we move forward to the next point in time and prepare for the next description.

I sum up so far. Manuel is our obvious guide to the world of *La busca*. As he moves, so we move with him; as he observes, so we too are invited to observe. We start, then, from Manuel's viewpoint. Gradually, however, the author takes over, supplementing the here-and-now with his own knowledge, his own observations and, very especially, his own guidance. Baroja does not, then, like many young novelists of the 1950s who so admired *La busca*, attempt a cine-camera and tape-recorder transcription of reality with all its commonplaces and its trivialities. Condensation, selection, supplementation, highlighting and emotive colouring all play an important part in his writing. There is ample further illustration of all this in the scenes that follow: the siesta in the Corralón, Vidal's account of the Piratas, the meeting with El Bizco and his gang and their subsequent marauding around the Casa del Cabrero and along the edge of the Manzanares.[12]

In these scenes there is also a noteworthy new element: when Vidal announces that they are going off to meet the Piratas, Manuel ceases for a moment to be a mere observer and takes part in a conversation with his cousin. His contribution is confined to three short questions: '¿Adónde?', 'Pero ¿qué piratas?' and '¿Y por qué los llaman así?' (p. 284). He passes, then, here, from his role as observer to his closely related role as an elicitor of information — another means of furthering observation, both his and the reader's —, and Vidal's reply serves as a preparation for the meeting with the gang. Similarly, when they are later down by the Casa del Cabrero, Manuel asks three further questions ('¿Hacen pucheros?', 'Pues ¿por qué son puchereras?' and 'Pero ¿esas chicas?', p. 285) which prompt further information and, by the resulting contrast with Manuel's naivety, serve to emphasize the insensitivity and brutishness of the other members of the gang. Manuel, at this point, also makes his most positive contribution so far: 'Manuel contempló al Bizco con desprecio.' We are touching here on another of his functions: to guide us in our emotive response to what is described (in the same way that Ignacio and Leandro earlier

---

[12] In the description of the children in the Casa del Cabrero there is an especially notable example of Baroja's darkened vision and greater subjectivity in the 1903 version. Since it involves a change in a basic fact (about whether the children made a noise or not) it offers not merely evidence but actual proof that Baroja was not an objective writer:

1903   Pululaba una nube de chiquillos desnudos, de color de tierra, la mayoría negros, algunos rubios, de ojos azules, *que gritaban y chillaban*. Había también unas cuantas chiquillas de diez á catorce años, que el Bizco y Vidal persiguieron por el patio. Corrían las chicas medio desnudas, *riendo* y dando agudos chillidos. (*El Globo*, 12 March; my italics)

1904   Pululaba una nube de chiquillos desnudos, de color de tierra, la mayoría negros, algunos rubios, de ojos azules. *Como si sintieran ya la degradación de su miseria, aquellos chicos no alborotaban ni gritaban.*

Unas cuantas chiquillas de diez a catorce años charlaban en grupo. El Bizco y Vidal y los demás las persiguieron por el patio. Corrían las chicas medio desnudas, *insultándoles* y chillando. (p. 284; my italics)

guided us in our response to Leandra's immoral observations). Of course it also reveals something of his character and in a Galdós novel this would be important. It is so far not obviously important in *La busca*. So far at least there is little evidence that Manuel's character either reveals itself in action or influences events.

From the Casa del Cabrero the gang go on to the mortuary and then along the edge of the Manzanares and on to some primitive shacks of filthy matting. El Bizco pilfers a piece of cod, whereupon 'Manuel sintió un miedo horrible' (another reader-guiding emotive response) and they all run off as someone approaches: 'Echaron todos los de la cuadrilla a correr por el paseo del Canal'. The inevitable description follows:

> Se veía Madrid envuelto en una nube de polvo, con sus casas amarillentas. Las altas vidrieras relucían a la luz del sol poniente.

But there is a difference from the other descriptions so far referred to: there is no introductory reference back to Manuel or to any other person; the description is introduced not by 'Manuel veía' or 'Veían', but by the more detached 'Se veía', and our gaze is directed now not into the anthill of human degradation but outwards towards Madrid and its distant houses and its windows glinting in the evening sun.

As the gang enter the Corralón and Manuel and Vidal go off upstairs, Ignacio is beating his wife and Vidal directs his cousin back to the Calle del Aguila. There is further oscillation between action and description of the surrounding scene ('Manuel siguió el camino indicado. Hacía un calor horrible...') and the boy finally reaches the Calle del Aguila. The closing paragraphs of the chapter are among the finest in the book and merit quotation at length:

> Cuando llegó Manuel frente a la escalera de la calle del Aguila, anochecía. Se sentó a descansar un rato en el Campillo de Gil Imón. Veíase desde allá arriba el campo amarillento, cada vez más sombrío con la proximidad de la noche, y las chimeneas y las casas perfiladas con dureza en el horizonte. El cielo, azul y verde arriba, se inyectaba de rojo a

ras de la tierra, se oscurecía y tomaba colores siniestros, rojos
cobrizos, rojos de púrpura.

Asomaban por encima de las tapias las torrecitas y cipreses
del cementerio de San Isidro; una cúpula redonda se
destacaba recortada en el aire; en su remate se erguía un
angelote con las alas desplegadas, como presto para levantar
el vuelo sobre el fondo incendiado y sangriento de la tarde.

Por encima de las nubes estratificadas del crepúsculo
brillaba una pálida estrella en una gran franja verde, y en el
vago horizonte, animado por la última palpitación del día, se
divisaban, inciertos, montes lejanos.

In the first line the oscillation between action (preterites) and
description (imperfects) continues, but from 'Veíase' onwards
— another indication of detachment from the sordid world in
which Manuel is immersed — everything is descriptive and in the
imperfect tense: the yellow countryside of late summer growing
gradually darker with the approach of night, the chimneys and
the houses starkly outlined against the horizon, and the sky,
serenely blue and green above but tinged with sinister reds and
coppers and purples at ground level. And the sinister element is
taken up again in the reference to the graveyard with its
'torrecitas' and its 'cipreses', and the church dome with its
despective 'angelote' that seems to preside over the fiery
holocaust of the earth. And way above the clouds a single star
shines palely amidst the distant green of the sky — serenely
detached and impassive to the human sordidness and baseness
and degradation that have been the main theme of the chapter
— and as the horizon gives its last quiver of life, vague forms of
distant hills are seen, scarcely, in the distance.

The passage has been much developed from its 1903 version
and comparison with that version is revealing.[13]A number of

---

13   Cuando llegó Manuel á la escalera de la calle del Aguila anochecía. Desde
      su parte alta se veía el cielo rojizo á rás de tierra, verde más arriba. El campo
      amarillo iba ensombreciéndose.
         Sobre el fondo rojo del cielo, en el cementerio de San Isidro, entre
      torrecitas y cipreses que asomaban por encima de las tapias, se destacaba una
      cúpula redonda y sobre ella un angelote con las alas levantadas que parecía
      que iba á echar á volar.
         Hacia Poniente se divisaban inciertos montes lejanos, sobre los últimos
      resplandores cobrizos de la tarde, que iban apagándose. (*El Globo*, 12 March
      1903)

changes strike one especially: the indication that Manuel 'se sentó a descansar un rato', which justifies a longer description and, more importantly, encourages a more contemplative approach to the scene; the more impressionistic technique ('rojos cobrizos, rojos de púrpura') with the corresponding elimination of intellectualizing subordinate clauses (especially in the second paragraph, singularly clumsy and unlyrical in the 1903 version, with the climax of anti-lyricism in the final words, 'que parecía que iba á echar á volar': double subordination, prosy wording and ugly sounds and rhythms); the retention of the psychological object — in each case, here, the grammatical subject — after verbs inviting perception ('Veíase... el campo amarillo', 'Asomaban... las torrecitas', 'en el vago horizonte... montes lejanos'), a means of exploiting both rhythm and word order to give an impression of distance, to emphasize the object observed and to bring out associated emotive resonances; a more vivid contrast between the serenity and the destruction-threatening aspects of the sky by the development of both these planes; an effect of greater dynamism produced by the use of words with human or possibly human connotations ('sombrío', 'dureza', 'se inyectaba', 'tomaba', 'siniestros', 'se erguía', 'sangriento', 'animado por la última palpitación'). In short, the 1904 version is clearly more vivid, more emotive, more lyrical and, though Baroja himself might have rejected the term, more literary. Contrary to common critical belief Baroja can be a superb stylist. The evidence of the above changes suggests that he also wanted to be.

* * * * * *

I have touched in this chapter on some of the most important features of Baroja's writing. The guiding thread of my study has been the function of the central protagonist. In fact, Manuel has four functions.

In the first place, he is the essential linear link between scenes, characters and episodes. He enters a house and the house is immediately described; he sits down at table and the people

around him are described; he is present at a conversation and
highlights of the conversation are reproduced; he goes out into
the patio and the people there are described.... Where Manuel
goes, we go too. And as we saw in the previous chapter, this is
true of the novel as a whole and, indeed, of the entire trilogy.
Whether only a moment passes between one episode and the
next, or several months, Manuel is there as the essential link.
Except for the opening pages of the novel, before his arrival in
Madrid — the least Barojan and most Galdosian pages in the
novel —, Manuel is with us constantly. As we follow him in his
andanzas we perceive what he perceives.

This brings us to Manuel's second function: that of an open-
eyed observer of the world around him. As he observes, so we
also are invited to observe, 'En la comida', we are told, 'Manuel
escuchó, sin terciar en la conversación', which is exactly what we
ourselves do. Similarly, a few paragraphs later, we find him
observing El Bizco 'con tranquilidad' and we as readers are
allowed to share his observation: 'La frente estrecha, la nariz
roma, los labios abultados, la piel pecosa y el pelo rojo y duro, le
daban el aspecto de un mandrilo grande y rubio.' In the details
of a single passage as in the progression of the whole trilogy
Manuel is the reader's shifting observation point.

Also — and this is Manuel's third function — by asking
questions he elicits information and thereby prompts further
observation. We have seen two series of examples in these pages,
each composed of three short questions: with the first series he
prompts Vidal to set the scene for the imminent meeting with El
Bizco and his gang; with the second he encourages El Bizco and
the others to reveal more both about themselves and about the
women in the Casa del Cabrero.

Finally, by his emotive responses — most commonly
responses of disgust — he guides us in our reaction to the
various scenes presented. We have noted two examples in these
pages: 'Manuel contempló al Bizco con desprecio' and 'Manuel
sintió un miedo horrible'.

Of these four functions the second and third (observer and
elicitor of information) can be brought together, for they both

serve observation. We are thus left with three notable functions that we can epitomize in the words *linearity*, *observation* and *emotivity*.

But these are not only Manuel's most notable functions; as was glimpsed in the previous chapter and has been seen more clearly in the present one, they are also the three most notable features of Baroja's novel-writing. Thus, the basic structure of the narrative is linear and episodic, with a simple linear progression sustained by Manuel's presence and Baroja's preterites, and a widening out at successive moments into observation and descriptive imperfects. But the descriptions, however real and vivid, are scarcely objective and we must reject this favourite word of writers on *La busca*. Selection, condensation, highlighting, supplementation and emotive colouring all play an important part. Thus, in the description of Salomé and Leandra and their respective husbands there is notably less emphasis on the pleasant partner than on the unpleasant one, and much of Baroja's description in this particular passage — most of it if one accepts that Salomé's husband is absent — depends not on observation but on supplementation. And what is supplemented — what is added to here-and-now observation — is evidence of animality so that even the wretched pairing of the two couples offends our moral sensitivity. Similarly, in what follows, the insipid trivia of family conversation are omitted, the preliminaries of a more promisingly degrading exchange are summed up in two or three telling lines, and we are presented in the dialogue with only the highlights, with Ignacio and Leandro close at hand to guide our disgust. Life, for Baroja, is brutal, bestial, degrading; people are brutal, bestial, degraded. It is this dark, essentially emotive vision of life that he most commonly communicates in *La busca* — by what he selects from the reality that Manuel perceives, by what he condenses, by what he highlights and by what he adds. And yet the final paragraphs of the pages that we have examined suggest that he cherishes, too, a purer vision — of a world, if necessary, purged of humans by some cosmic holocaust —, a vision of serenity and calm that shines like a star, but faintly, in the far distance.

Most of the rest of this study will serve to develop these various points.

4. Linearity: guiding characters

Characters in *La busca* fall broadly into two groups: the few who carry the story line and the many who are observed from different points in the story line. We are concerned in this chapter with the former. Manuel is the clearest example. Except in the opening pages of the novel he is our constant observation post, seeing but rarely seen. Thus, of all the characters in the novel he is perhaps the only one of whom Baroja offers no physical description, and his character is determined throughout by the author's need for a drifting observer whose view-point the reader can readily accept. Basically he is an ingenuous *vagabundo* — an appropriate guide to the world of the 'hombre humilde y errante' (V,158) who wrote the novel —, able to conform to successive environments but with enough of his mother's morality to preserve detachment from them and enough of his father's temper to ensure his periodic removal from one environment to another. For the rest, his experiences are simply thrust upon him by others.

When the novel opens, Manuel has spent two years living with relatives in the province of Soria — much to his distaste. 'Lo peor era que ni su tío ni la mujer de su tío le mostraron afecto, sino indiferencia' (p. 265). Besides, Manuel, 'perezoso e indolente', dislikes both school and study, the local schoolmaster sees him as 'un holgazán aventurero y vagabundo' (p. 265) and his uncle has finally decided that he is wasting his time and should go off to Madrid to learn a trade. Manuel's easy acceptance of the rigours of the journey, the lack of affection shown to him, his sense of awe at the sight of Almazán, 'enorme, tristísimo', his 'angustia' on reaching Madrid and the frankness and honesty and 'sencillez' — and lack of animosity and self-delusion — that he reveals in his replies to his mother on his arrival all serve to dispel any serious misgivings that the reader might have about him. By the time he reaches Doña Casiana's boarding-house we are already close to the view that Roberto will express about him almost seventeen years later, near the end of the final volume of the trilogy: 'muy buen chico; pero sin voluntad, sin energía' (p. 632).

This resemblance between Manuel as he is at the beginning and at the end of the trilogy points to an important feature of Baroja's view of human character. For better or for worse people are what they are. They evolve little. There is therefore little evidence in his novels of interaction between one character and another or between a character and his circumstances. Manuel will remain throughout a rather passive — and generally impassive — observer of the world around him. It is less the observer who matters in Baroja than the world he observes.

And Manuel's observations start immediately: 'Manuel se dedicó a observar a los huéspedes. Era el día siguiente al complot, y doña Violante y sus niñas estaban hurañas y malhumoradas [etc.]' (p. 267). And as Manuel observes, so also the reader observes. Because of his remarkable 'facultades de acomodación' (p. 269) Manuel feels, within a week of his arrival, that he has always lived there and he is able to give appropriate expression to his continuing '[espíritu de] holgazán aventurero y vagabundo'. Despite his generally easy-going temperament, however, he finally comes to blows with one of the guests and is expelled. Roberto gives him the support that others deny and Manuel shakes his hand 'muy agradecido'.

We find the same basic characteristics in the next stage of his Madrid experiences, down in the low quarter. 'Se conforma pronto', observes Ignacio when Manuel is told he will be staying there. 'Sí', replies his mother; 'todo lo toma con calma' (p. 279). But he finds the first morning's work 'pesadísima'; 'el estar tanto tiempo quieto le resultó insoportable' (p. 280). These two qualities — on the one hand, Manuel's ability to conform; on the other hand, his dislike of restraints on his freedom — reappear a couple of pages later: 'Al principio, la monotonía en el trabajo y la sujeción atormentaban a Manuel: pero pronto se acostumbró a una cosa y otra, y los días le parecieron más cortos y la labor menos penosa' (p. 282).[14] Meanwhile, of course, he continues to act as the essential link between the different scenes presented and as the reader's shifting view-point: scene and conversations in the cobbler's shop, scene and conversations in Ignacio's house, wanderings round the poor quarter with the Piratas, scenes and characters in the Corralón, a trip to the Doctrina with Roberto... La Petra would doubtless have considered the experiences even less 'edificantes' than those that preoccupied her in Doña Casiana's boarding-house, but Manuel adapts to life in the poor quarter as he earlier adapted to life at Doña Casiana's: 'A los dos o tres meses de estancia en el Corralón, Manuel se hallaba tan acostumbrado a su trabajo y a su vida, que no comprendía que pudiese hacer otra cosa' (p. 295). Besides, he finds here something of the companionship that was lacking in Soria and for which he was grateful to Roberto, while at the same time being able to indulge his spirit of adventure. And yet, despite his delight in 'correrías' with El Bizco and his gang, his moral sense keeps him somewhat uninvolved in their activities and his 'odio y repugnancia por el Bizco' serves Baroja nicely at one point (p. 296) as a means of transition to the description of less tragically sombre, though equally picturesque, characters such as the Rebolledos and the Aristas. This oscillation between the depiction of sombre, bestial creatures and the presentation of characters who are mainly picturesque or eccentric is repeated in the following two chapters (II, V-VI) in which Manuel escorts Roberto, and the duality is generally overlooked by commentators intent on emphasizing Baroja's purely pessimistic vision. We shall return to the point in

[14] In the 1904 version Baroja pays far more attention than he did in 1903 to Manuel's situation, in particular to the duality of *sujeción* and *vagabundaje*, and most examples of authorial guidance on this — including those quoted in the above paragraph — were added in 1904. Apart from the greater light that is thereby thrown on Manuel, it seems clear that Baroja was seeking also — and more importantly — to justify the basic construction and progression of the novel: with periods of *sujeción* to allow a pause for observation and description, and outbursts of *vagabundaje* to ensure Manuel's periodic removal from one area of experience to another. In miniature we have seen something similar in the author's characteristic interplay of descriptive imperfects and action preterites.

a later chapter.

Leandro's death and Ignacio's illness precipitate Manuel and
the reader into further experiences of Madrid life and we see in
turn 'el drama del tío Patas', life in a bakery, and a succession of
scenes of *golfería* and petty crime: 'La historia del tío Patas era
verdaderamente interesante' (p. 325) and Baroja takes
advantage of Manuel's presence to recount it; 'La vida allí [en la
tahona] era horriblemente penosa' (p. 326) and Baroja recounts
the details; '¡Si te digo que es una vida de *chipendi*!' proclaims
Vidal and again the point is amply illustrated (p. 331). And
always Manuel is poised between contradictory pressures: he
would like to enjoy — and even to lead — a better life, but that
would seem to involve restrictions on his 'instinto antisocial de
vagabundo' (p. 347). 'Acostumbrado a los paseos diarios por las
rondas, le desesperaba tal inmovilidad' (p. 325; a 1904
addition). Besides, he finds indifference to him among his
workmates in the bakery — in contrast to the companionship
that he enjoys in his wanderings round Madrid. But whatever his
wishes may be, Manuel is still, above all, a conformist. He leaves
Ignacio's because he has to leave; he works for Tío Patas
because his mother places him there and he stays there until she
takes him away; he works in the bakery because his mother
transfers him there and he remains there until he falls ill and has
to return to Doña Casiana's. Manuel rarely guides his own
destiny; life is simply something that happens to him. One of the
rare occasions on which he does influence his own movements is
when he attempts to have 'una explicación a solas' with Doña
Casiana's niece and is expelled from the boarding-house for the
second time (pp. 329-30). Yet even there he is rehabilitated
somewhat by the later discovery of 'explicación' tendencies in
the girl herself (p. 333).

After leaving the boarding-house Manuel calls on Salomé,
and afterwards,

Al encontrarse en la ronda, lo primero que se le ocurrió a
Manuel fue que no debía ir al puente de Toledo, ni mucho
menos a la carretera de Andalucía, porque allí era fácil que se
encontrase con Vidal o con el Bizco. Pensó así,

efectivamente, y, a pesar de esto, bajó hacia el puente, echó
una ojeada por los cajones, y viendo que allí no estaban sus
amigos, siguió por el Canal, atravesó el Manzanares [etc.]. (p.
331)

And of course he does meet Vidal and El Bizco, and when Vidal
proposes forming a 'cuadrilla' Manuel, though reluctant ('de
mala gana'), allows himself to be included. But he fears the sort
of life that the other two lead and no sooner has the 'Sociedad de
los Tres' been formed than we read, on the same page, 'Tenía
que resolverse a dar a su existencia un nuevo giro; pero ¿cuál?
Eso es lo que no sabía' (p. 333). At this point he hears of his
mother's illness and returns to Doña Casiana's to be with her as
she dies. He is much moved by her death and thinks and suffers
as he has never thought or suffered before. But on the day after
the funeral he leaves Doña Casiana's and joins a group of
urchins:

> Manuel se tendió perezosamente al sol; sentía el bienestar
> de hallarse libre por completo de preocupaciones, de ver el
> cielo azul extendiéndose hasta el infinito. Aquel bienestar le
> llevó a un sueño profundo. (III,II; p. 336)

His mother, so far, has been the principal organizer of his life;
now he is free from any guidance that she might have imposed.
Brief experiences with the urchins are succeeded by a short
chance encounter with Roberto, and, after a week sleeping in the
open, Manuel again joins Vidal and El Bizco. After they have
cheated El Pastiri of his ill-gotten gains, 'a Manuel no le pareció
tan mal el comienzo de la vida de golfería' (p. 346), but on the
following day his mother's morality — and his own sense of a
possible better existence — reasserts itself: 'Yo no sirvo para
esto', he thinks; 'Ideó mil cosas, la mayoría irrealizables;
imaginó proyectos complicados'; Vidal and El Bizco, he feels,
are lucky because they do not have his misgivings. 'A pesar de
sus escrúpulos y remordimientos, el verano lo pasó Manuel
protegido por El Bizco y Vidal' (p. 347). The irony of the
juxtaposition is delightful and again the emphasis is on Manuel's
inability to influence his own life. When he finally breaks with
Vidal it is because he has to: because Vidal, his mentor, leaves

him and Manuel is turned out of the house they shared.

After several weeks living rough Manuel is picked up by Señor Custodio, the rubbish collector, and goes to live with him and his wife. 'Los primeros días en casa del señor Custodio parecieron a Manuel de demasiada sujeción; pero como en la vida del trapero hay mucho de vagabundaje, pronto se acostumbró a ella' (p. 359). One notes the continuing duality of *sujeción* and *vagabundaje*. Moreover, as in the Corralón, he comes to find something attractive in the apparently unattractive setting of Custodio's house and even becomes enthusiastic about the life he leads there. Besides, he glimpses again the possibility of affection (p. 361). But when Custodio's daughter, Justa, trifles with his feelings, he is overcome with 'pensamientos negros y tristes, la idea de la inutilidad de su vida' (p. 365), and these are succeeded by 'la ira y la desesperación más rabiosa' (p. 366) when she brings home a suitor. Despite Custodio's influence on him, Manuel's 'instintos aventureros persistían'; 'pensaba marcharse a América, en hacerse marinero, en alguna cosa por el estilo' (p. 367). But only 'pensaba'. Finally, overcome with envy and anger, he attacks El Carnicerín at a wedding reception — the father's streak that Petra feared —, is ejected and goes off crying with rage and shame, with thoughts of the frightful death he will one day inflict on his enemy. 'Y luego generalizaba su odio y pensaba que la sociedad entera se ponía en contra de él y no trataba más que de martirizarle y de negarle todo' (p. 370). He will oppose society, then, and join El Bizco, since he feels he cannot now return to Custodio's. But though he immediately meets El Bizco, he does not join him. Instead, he vents his anger on a thug who is bullying a young boy, reflects again on his life and thinks with hatred of El Carnicerín 'porque le arrebataba su dicha, le imposibilitaba vivir en el rincón donde únicamente encontró algún cariño y alguna protección' (p. 372; a 1904 addition). The novel ends with his resolution to be one of life's 'trabajadores' rather than one of its 'noctámbulos'.

And of course he may be. On the other hand, he may not. Unforeseen circumstances will doubtless play a part. And if there were to be no unforeseen circumstances? The fact is that we simply do not know. What we do know is that Manuel's reflections and resolutions have very little influence on his actions. He reveals a basis of morality but it is difficult to see how this can be sufficient to overcome his 'instinto antisocial de vagabundo' or the associated distaste for a life of 'sujeción' — unless, of course, he can summon up a certain amount of will power. But, on the evidence so far, will power seems to be notably lacking. At the end of the book as at the beginning Manuel is still basically a drifter, adapting himself chameleon-like to whatever environment he finds himself in. Consequently, to say of Manuel's future, 'And if there were to be no unforeseen circumstances?' is a particularly futile hypothesis. Life always presents unforeseen circumstances, especially life as portrayed by Baroja, and Manuel's future will depend on them. The question then is: what circumstances will present themselves? Unless there are positive influences to counteract his 'instinto antisocial y vagabundo' his future does not seem very promising. But there will be such influences and the initial source of them is to be found in *La busca*: in Roberto Hasting, the student, part English, part Spanish, who holds up to Manuel, in his various appearances, an image of will and determination in face of adversity. It is his character and function that we must now consider.

Roberto serves less exclusively than Manuel to carry the story line. Like other characters in *La busca* he is also much observed from Manuel's successive standpoints. His main functions, it seems, are the following:

1. Through the story of his quest for a denied inheritance he introduces a typically Barojan element of intrigue, mystery and suspense.

2. In his alleged quest for that inheritance he serves, like Manuel, as a link between successive scenes and thereby enables Baroja to add further knots to the basically rope-and-knots progression of the novel.[15]

[15] The above observation is based exclusively on the internal evidence of *La busca* 1904. The 1903-4 revision shows that it needs supplementing. Roberto did not exist in *La busca* 1903; on the other hand, most of the episodes in

3. In the determination with which he pursues his quest he serves as a notably contrasting foil to Manuel.

4. In his seriousness and sense of honour he offers a notable contrast to the frivolity and the low moral standards of many of Manuel's other contacts.

5. Because of these qualities of determination, seriousness and sense of honour he serves — to a certain extent in *La busca* and increasingly in *Mala hierba* and *Aurora roja* — as a representative of Baroja's own standards and a mouthpiece of his views.

6. Finally, in *Mala hierba* and *Aurora roja* he will serve to give the feckless Manuel periodic help to better fortunes, which in turn opens up two possibilities: firstly, descriptions of further aspects of Madrid life, and secondly, Manuel's response to his successive positions in the light of his basically vagabond spirit. Of these six functions the second, as supplemented by the footnote, is the most important in *La busca*, followed closely by the third and fourth, and it is these that I shall emphasize in my survey.

Roberto first appears among the guests in Doña Casiana's boarding-house. 'El estudiante rubio, con sus ojos de acero' — both generally favourable physical characteristics in Baroja's world — is somewhat aloof from the other guests: indifferent to their 'juerga', 'embebido en sus pensamientos' and scornful of Celia's taunt that he has no blood in his veins (p. 271). But beneath his 'habitual frialdad' there is love and melancholy (p. 272), a notable capacity for anger, especially at injustice (p. 277) and, very especially, a clear view of where he is going and the importance of ambition in life (p. 273). Probings by a fellow guest on these last points prompt Roberto to reveal

which he becomes involved in 1904 (for example, the visit to the Doctrina and to La Blasa's tavern) and most of the characters he meets (Señor Zurro, El Tabuenca, Don Alonso...) did exist but as even more self-contained and static elements, unrelated to anyone's quest for an inheritance. Roberto, then, not only enables Baroja to add knots to his narration; more importantly, he joins with Manuel to connect up already existing knots, both episodes and characters, and, at the same time, to integrate these into some semblance of a developing action centred on his quest for an inheritance. Roberto, then, plays an important constructional role in the 1904 revised version and the manner of his introduction confirms his linear function.

to Don Telmo his conviction that one day he will inherit a fortune. For the moment, however, Manuel and the reader manage to overhear only fragments of his story (pp. 274-5). When Roberto learns that Manuel, expelled from the boarding-house, will be living in the low quarter of Madrid, he is interested:

> —Oye —le dijo a Manuel—, si conoces algún sitio raro por barrios bajos donde vaya mala gente, avísame; iré contigo. (p. 277)

In fact, it is Roberto himself who takes the initiative: a few weeks later when he visits Manuel at the *zapatería* and takes him off to the Friday doling out of religious instruction — and sometimes charity — at the Doctrina. There are some excellent descriptions of human degradation, both physical and psychological. There are reflections on the inhumanity of men and women, both rich and poor. There are lively and spicy fragments of dialogue. There are some typically Barojan contrasts between teeming, sordid humanity and serene, impassive nature. But there is nothing there relevant to Roberto's quest, and the momentary presence of Don Telmo's niece adds nothing but a touch of intrigue and mystery. Nor is it clear why Manuel himself was taken along, except as the reader's observation post. '—A ti te chocarán—dijo Roberto—estas maniobras mías; pero no te extrañarán cuando te diga que busco aquí dos mujeres: una, pobre, que puede hacerme rico; otra, rica, que quizás me hiciera pobre' (p. 292). Manuel, doubtful about the student's mental state, cannot suppress an ironic smile. Nor can the reader. But Roberto is not the sort of person to be discouraged by the scepticism of others:

> De repente, Roberto se paró, y poniendo la mano en el hombro de Manuel le dijo:
> —Hazme caso, porque es la verdad. Si quieres hacer algo en la vida, no creas en la palabra imposible. Nada hay imposible para una voluntad enérgica. Si tratas de disparar una flecha, apunta muy alto, lo más alto que puedas; cuanto más alto apuntes, más lejos irá.
> Manuel miró a Roberto con extrañeza y se encogió de hombros. (p. 294)

The contrast between the two characters is clear and similar contrasts will appear again and again. Whereas Manuel and others drift, Roberto steers a fixed, well-mapped route. Of course, he is part English and Baroja responded warmly to contemporary notions that the Anglo-Saxon — and the Germanic race in general — was superior to the Latin race. Amidst a general atmosphere of apathy and stagnation Baroja's novels present a number of dynamic men of resolution and action. They are most commonly either English (or were educated in England) or natives of Baroja's own Basque Country. The contrast between Roberto and Manuel, I repeat, is clear; equally clear, I suggest, is the absence of any influence of the one on the other. Characters in Baroja are almost completely self-contained. The fact that Baroja could add Roberto in the 1903-4 revision without any accompanying change to Manuel's character is clear proof of this.

As Manuel prepared to leave Doña Casiana's, Roberto asked him to let him know if he came across any 'sitio raro' frequented by 'mala gente'; towards the end of the Doctrina chapter he made a similar request: 'siempre que vayas a algún sitio donde se reúna gente pobre o de mala vida, avísame' (p. 294). When Leandro invites his cousin on a trip round bars in the poor quarter, Manuel thinks of Roberto and they ask him along. Roberto appears with his cousin Fanny, a delightful caricature of what generations of Spaniards have seen as the typical English woman: scraggy, big-boned, unfeminine, eccentric and notably horsy. 'Mi prima', says Roberto, 'tiene gana de ver algo de la vida pobre de estos barrios' (p. 299). They start by showing her the Corralón. 'Aquí miseria es lo único que se ve', comments Leandro. '¡Oh, sí, sí!' replies Fanny in evident delight. They go on to visit an evil-smelling, oil-lit tavern in the slum quarter of Las Injurias. There are men playing cards; women huddled together on the floor, some of them with babies in their arms or dozing with a cigarette hanging from their mouths; worn-out prostitutes; children deformed and diseased. The atmosphere is one of bad temper, hostility, aggression, human degradation. When Fanny gives a five-peseta coin (a thousand-peseta note by

today's standards) to one of the gypsy women for her *churumbel*
they decide it would be safer to leave. Outside it is raining. In the
narrow alley-ways their feet sink into filth and slime. It is an
extremely vivid chapter. But it has no relevance to Roberto's
search for his denied inheritance — or to novel progression in a
Galdosian sense. It is completely self-contained, like many a
chapter in the novels of Dickens whom Baroja so admired. More
specifically, it is *turismo de barrio bajo*: the stimulation of
strong responses by means of violent scenes; characteristically
powerful knots added to a characteristically slim story-line.

The next chapter takes place a few months later and again
Roberto is there. This time he has come to Manuel for
something specifically related to his quest: he wants to trace a
former circus artist called Rosa. She used to lodge nearby and
Roberto believes that Señor Zurro, who lives in the Corralón,
may be able to help him to find her. Señor Zurro is not able to
help but he refers Roberto to El Tabuenca, with whom,
somewhat incidentally, Roberto comes to blows. The muleteer
landlord intervenes and refers Roberto to Don Alonso, who goes
round cafés at night playing a phonograph. As Roberto and
Manuel have a meal together in the café where they hope to meet
Don Alonso, Roberto again apostrophizes his amazed friend on
the subject of will and energy: 'se tiene un caudal de voluntad en
billetes, en onzas, en grandes unidades, y se necesita la energía
en céntimos, en perros chicos' (p. 305). Don Alonso arrives —
an eccentric Dickensian character who reminds us that Baroja is
not interested only in slum life — but he is unable to help.
Baroja does, however, allow him to fill ten pages of normal
volume size with a picturesque account of his circus travels in the
New World. As Don Alonso leaves, Roberto himself makes the
obvious point: 'Nada, no se averigua nada [...]. Vaya, adiós;
hasta otro día' (p. 310). Another blank for Roberto; another
series of knots for Baroja; nothing that one could traditionally
call progression for either of them.

Roberto appears only once more in *La busca*, six chapters
later. A year has passed. Roberto's fortunes, like Manuel's, are
at their lowest point and the two friends meet, destitute, in the

beggars' food queue at the María Cristina barracks. Manuel feels that his life lacks direction: 'no sabía qué hacer, ni qué camino seguir' (p. 339). Roberto, in the past, has felt something similar: 'la esterilidad de mi vida' and the lack of 'una ocasión y un fin para emanciparse de esta existencia mezquina'. Indeed, his quest for an inheritance, he tells Manuel, was undertaken originally 'sin esperanza ninguna, sólo como una gimnasia de la voluntad' (p. 341). On the one hand, then, there is Manuel, with his acceptance of life's pointlessness; on the other hand, Roberto, with his determination to forge some sort of aim in life. In a context of Galdosian realism one would look for evidence of interaction between these two responses; in a Barojan context one suspects that there will be none. Indeed, the very disparity between Roberto's talk of his grandiose inheritance and his present real-life situation convinces Manuel that the student is out of his mind (pp. 339, 340, 341):

> Manuel encontraba necio estar hablando de tanta grandeza cuando ni uno ni otro tenían para comer, y pretextando una ocupación se despidió de Roberto. (p. 343)

Baroja, then, throws away an excellent opportunity to show character interaction and development.[16] All he had to do was to offer some slight evidence that Roberto's 'voluntad y decisión' were producing results — just enough to dispel that barrier of irony that prevents Manuel from responding positively to Roberto's example. But character development and interaction, it seems, were not Baroja's aim. What he is here concerned with is a philosophical and psychological problem: How does one respond to life's pointlessness? Does one accept it and succumb or does one set up against it one's own personal life-lie? Does one remain 'en el fondo del abismo' or does one forge a faith 'con razón, sin razón o contra la razón' (Unamuno)? We are a long way from the abstracted puppets of Unamuno's novels, but Baroja's protagonists are involved in a similar existential dialectic.

Alongside Manuel who is our constant guide and Roberto

---

[16] See below, p. 102-3, for further evidence of how Baroja deliberately does this.

who joins in periodically to supplement the journey one has to mention a third character, Manuel's younger cousin, Vidal. He is less obviously a guide and justification for successive scenes than Manuel and Roberto and he is more obviously integrated into the surrounding landscape of what is described. Nevertheless, the frequency of his appearance, the way in which he serves, both in *La busca* and in *Mala hierba*, to introduce Manuel and the reader to specific areas of experience and, finally, his presence as a counterbalance to Roberto make it desirable to consider him, at least briefly, in the present chapter.

During the first lunch-break after Manuel's arrival at the *zapatería* he proceeds to tell Manuel about the delights of the area and he offers him a girl friend. On the following Sunday he collects Manuel from the Calle del Aguila and, as we saw in the previous chapter, escorts him first to the Corralón and then on to join El Bizco and the Piratas. Once Manuel himself has moved to the Corralón, Vidal and he go to work together every morning. 'Y constantemente, al ir y al venir, la conversación de Manuel y de Vidal versaba sobre lo mismo: las mujeres, el dinero' (p. 295). Manuel dislikes El Bizco's company but, weak-willed as usual, 'no se decidía a oponerse a lo que pensaba Vidal' (p. 296) and he goes along with him. 'El lazo de unión entre Manuel y el Bizco era Vidal' (p. 296). Similarly, it is Vidal who, eighteen months later, acts as the focus of attraction for Manuel and causes him to join up again with the *golfos* and *randas* of the outskirts and to embark on a life of petty crime. When Vidal decides to break with El Bizco and join the claque of the Apolo Theatre and become involved with prostitutes, Manuel — and consequently also the reader — goes with him. The fact is that 'Manuel, en secreto, le envidiaba' (p. 352). When they eventually separate, it is because Vidal leaves Manuel. Here at least, it seems, there is evidence of influence. And yet it is minimal. What Vidal appeals to is Manuel's own basic 'instinto antisocial de vagabundo' and his need for companionship. Manuel remains throughout the open-eyed but essentially passive observer.

Manuel, then, our constant guide, is poised between

contrasting examples: on the one hand, Roberto who emphasizes the merits of will and energy but does not seem to be getting very far with them; on the other hand, Vidal, the *golfo*, who points the way to crime and seems to be making progress. Roberto — like Petra and Custodio, too, in their different ways — appeals to Manuel's basic morality and urges on him the need for some sort of *sujeción* (to priests and his 'superiores' in the case of Petra, p. 270; to 'sensatez', 'buen sentido', 'honor' and 'virtud' in the case of Custodio, pp. 361-2; to a personal plan of action in the case of Roberto, p. 341); Vidal, on the other hand, appeals to his desire for adventure and *vagabundaje*. The two possibilities, in so far as they are relevant to Manuel, are juxtaposed in the final moments of the novel: on the one hand, the 'trabajadores'; on the other hand, the 'noctámbulos'. Morality persists and, in thought at least, Manuel opts for the former. But the conflict is not yet over. In *Mala hierba* Manuel will be similarly poised: between Roberto on the one hand, with his advice to 'buscar, buscar y buscar [trabajo]' and then to 'trabajar hasta echar el alma por la boca' (p. 384) and, on the other hand, Alex and his fellow bohemians (in the early part of the novel) and Jesús and Vidal (in the later part) who offer various escapes from 'esta vida [de trabajo] tan igual y tan monótona' (p. 445). In *Aurora roja*, too: between Roberto, Salvadora and Ignacia, on the one hand, with their support for Manuel's idea of owning his own printing-shop, and his brother Juan, on the other hand, with his idealistic anarchism which comes close to landing them all in prison. Because of the sheer weight of domestic pressure perhaps, and by the manifest impracticality of his brother's anarchist ideals, it will finally be the bourgeois option of *sujeción* that will prevail and Manuel will accept his yoke without being much aware of it. Pushing a handcart, comments Baroja, is an excellent way of prompting thought. And as Manuel pushes his handcart to and from his printing-shop he fails to notice whether he is guiding it or it is guiding him. 'Así, en la vida, muchas veces no se sabe si es uno el que empuja los acontecimientos, o si son los acontecimientos los que le arrastran a uno' (p. 552).

It is a revealing observation and it is echoed throughout Baroja's writings. Already in his student years, he declared, he saw life as 'una corriente tumultuosa e inconsciente, donde los actores representaban una comedia que no comprendían' (VII, 598), and of himself he wrote, in 1917, 'A mí me gustaría evolucionar, pero ¿adónde? ¿Cómo? ¿En dónde se va a encontrar una dirección?' (V, 166). Life for Baroja has neither sense nor pattern nor significant direction. One is 'azotado por la necesidad, sin fin, sin objeto' (II, 110-11). If, like Roberto Hasting, one happens to be born with will and energy, one can perhaps impose a plan on one's life; if not, not. We are what we are and we can do nothing about it. Life for most of us is not something we control; it is something that happens to us, a series of experiences thrust upon us. The most one can do is approve or disapprove. Galdós's global novel construction is based on the assumption that there is interaction between characters and circumstances, that man can respond positively to his destiny; Baroja's linear construction is rooted in the belief that there is no such interaction, except for a basic reaction of disgust with life.

5. Observation: (1) Madrid low life

In the previous chapter we were concerned with the few characters who, between them, carry the story line; in the present chapter and Chapter 7 we shall be concerned with the question of what is observed from different points in the story line. 'Suponiendo que en mi obra literaria hay algo de valor', wrote Baroja with characteristic modesty, 'este valor creo que no es precisamente literario ni filosófico; es más bien psicológico y documental' (II, 229). His suggestion of 'valor psicológico' is perhaps questionable in the light of the previous chapter: psychologies are revealed and contrasted — often vividly —, but they are not probed deeply and they are not shown evolving, either in contact with one another or in contact with circumstances.

Except for the rather cavalier handling of chronology one need have no such reservation about Baroja's other, more frequently advanced suggestion. Like writers of the '98 Generation in general — and like Azorín, his closest friend among those writers, in particular — Baroja was a notable *excursionista*, an extremely sensitive observer of reality and a superb recorder of what he observed. Indeed, with Baroja as with others of his generation one suspects that there was perhaps a significant relationship between his feeling that life lacked direction and the eagerness with which he seized on here-and-now physical realities, as though these were life-rafts in the 'corriente tumultuosa e inconsciente' of existence. In this respect the following quotation seems relevant:

> De joven, y sin cultura, no iba yo a forjarme un concepto, una significación y un fin de la vida, cuando flotaba, y flota en el ambiente, la sospecha de si la vida no tendrá significado ni objeto; pero, sin proponérmelo y sin hacerlo de una manera expresa, marchaba a seguir la máxima del poeta latino: "Coge la flor de un día sin pensar demasiado en la de mañana." (VII, 566)

To seize on the flower of each successive present moment was apparently Baroja's unconscious response to life's lack of meaning and direction.

Baroja, then, made his descriptions 'por impresión directa' (VII, 1053): 'La mayoría de los personajes que han aparecido en mis novelas los he visto y conocido' (VII, 1075); 'El que lea mis libros, valgan lo que valgan literariamente, verá un paralelismo de los tipos descritos y de las escenas con los de la realidad' (VII, 430). Thus, with specific reference to *La busca* he has written:

El convivir durante algunos años con obreros panaderos, repartidores y gente pobre, el tener que acudir a veces a la taberna para llamar a un trabajador con frecuencia intoxicado, me impulsó a curiosear en los barrios bajos de Madrid, a pasear por las afueras y a escribir sobre la gente que está al margen de la sociedad [...].

Los cuadros que forman *La busca* y *Mala hierba*, que la sigue, son un conjunto de apuntes del natural, procedimiento que no es, sin duda, el mejor para producir una obra armónica y bien perfilada. (VII, 75)

In *Aventuras, inventos y mixtificaciones de Silvestre Paradox* (1901) there is an even more suggestive pointer to the sort of background that one imagines to the writing of *La busca*. When Paradox has Pelayo Huesca, an ex-policeman and ex-many-other-things, foisted on him as a servant-cum-secretary, he becomes fascinated by Pelayo's 'repertorio de historias de gente maleante a cuál más extrañas y sugestivas' and decides to use his knowledge of the underworld to write a serialized novel under the title *Los golfos de Madrid* or *El salón y la taberna* or *El mundo del vicio*. Don Pelayo then takes Paradox round the low quarter: 'Paradox tomó sus notas y siguió visitando, con su secretario, todos los garitos, buñolerías, chirlatas y madrigueras que conocía don Pelayo' (II, 108-11). This, one feels, must have been very similar to Baroja's own approach.

Successive scholars have drawn attention to the documentary realism of Baroja's novels and two scholars, Soledad Puértolas and Carmen del Moral Ruiz, have drawn extensively on background material of the Regency period (1885-1902) to demonstrate the point: Puértolas with quotation from the press of the period (*20*); Moral Ruiz with impressive documentation from newspapers, studies, reports and memoirs (*21*). In the pages that follow I am much indebted to their findings, which I have briefly supplemented by my own reading of the contemporary press.[17] My emphasis, however, is different from theirs: not so much on the <u>background panorama</u> of social <u>conditions from which</u> Baroja selected his material; far more on what he selected and how he presented it.

I start with living conditions. We can pass quickly over the 'morada casta y pura de doña Casiana' (p. 258) with its darkness, its griminess, its unpleasant smells and its poor food, remembering only that the Calle de Mesonero Romanos and its surroundings were very different then from now. The Gran Vía did not exist, the area was a maze of narrow streets, 'calles tortuosas y siniestras' (VII, 1117), and the Calle de Mesonero Romanos itself was 'llena de prostíbulos' (VII, 1120), one of which we glimpse across the street from Doña Casiana's boarding-house. In *La busca*, however, Baroja's main and most vivid emphasis is on conditions in the poor quarter. 'El madrileño que alguna vez, por casualidad, se encuentra en los barrios pobres próximos al Manzanares, hállase sorprendido ante el espectáculo de miseria y sordidez, de tristeza e incultura que ofrecen las afueras de Madrid' (p. 277). Streets are unsurfaced and ill lit and when it rains the whole area is converted into an 'hondonada, negra de cieno' (pp. 277, 302). It is to this other world of 'sombra oscura', of 'vida africana, de aduar' (p. 277) — the area of Madrid where there were most *casas de vecindad*, where rents were lowest, where there was the

[17] In the belief that, for reasons referred to above in Chapter 2, the Madrid press from 1899 to 1901 would be more relevant to *La busca* than the press of the years 1885-8 suggested by internal chronology and emphasized by Puértolas, I started my survey on 1 January 1899 with a single paper, *El Globo*. By the time I had reached March of that year I had such a profusion of evidence that it seemed pointless to proceed further. Consequently, what my own survey of the press lacked in breadth of coverage it gained in significance: that so much evidence should be available in a mere three-month span — and in a fairly conservative paper, too.

highest proportion of day labourers, hawkers and pedlars, and
where there was the highest mortality rate (Moral, pp. 77-95) —
that Manuel moves in Part II of *La busca*. The Corralón, it
seems, was a typical *casa de vecindad* of the sort that Philip
Hauser, in *Madrid bajo el punto de vista médico-social* (1902),
described as 'no aptas para ser habitadas por seres humanos'
(cit. Moral, p. 92). Baroja, in his *Memorias*, said that he based
his description of the Corralón on a specific house and
thereupon drew extensively on *La busca* to describe the house
(VII, 1128-9). In the 'patio grande', 'siempre sucio', rubbish was
thrown anywhere so that when it rained, 'como se obturaba casi
siempre la boca del sumidero, se producía una pestilencia
insoportable de la corrupción del agua negra que inundaba el
patio, y sobre la cual nadaban hojas de col y papeles pringosos'
(pp. 286-7). The surrounding galleries revealed differences
between one family and another, but the general impression was
one of dirt and misery ('Cada trozo de galería......
empobrecimiento moral', p. 287). The 'patio grande', however,
was the better part of the house. 'Un pasillo, lleno de
inmundicias', led on to a smaller patio, 'en el invierno
convertido en fétido pantano', where the rooms were much
cheaper: 'la mayoría eran de veinte y treinta reales; pero los
había de dos y tres pesetas al mes: chiscones oscuros, sin
ventilación alguna, construidos en los huecos de las escaleras y
debajo del tejado' (p. 287), the cheapest category of housing
indicated by Hauser in his survey (Table in Moral, p. 79).

As for the inhabitants — composed principally, says Hauser,
'de la clase jornalera, de empleados cesantes, de vendedores
ambulantes, de barrenderos y de traperos' (cit. Moral, p. 92) —,
Baroja writes:

> Era la Corrala un mundo en pequeño, agitado y febril, que
> bullía como una gusanera. Allí se trabajaba, se holgaba, se
> bebía, se ayunaba, se moría de hambre; allí se construían
> muebles, se falsificaban antigüedades, se zurcían bordados
> antiguos, se fabricaban buñuelos, se componían porcelanas
> rotas, se concertaban robos, se prostituían mujeres.
> Era la Corrala un microcosmos; se decía que, puestos en

hilera los vecinos, llegarían desde el arroyo de Embajadores a la plaza del Progreso; allí había hombres que lo eran todo y no eran nada: medio sabios, medio herreros, medio carpinteros, medio albañiles, medio comerciantes, medio ladrones.

Era, en general, toda la gente que allí habitaba gente descentrada, que vivía en el continuo aplanamiento producido por la eterna e irremediable miseria; muchos cambiaban de oficio, como un reptil de piel; otros no lo tenían; algunos peones de carpintero, de albañil, a consecuencia de su falta de iniciativa, de comprensión y de habilidad, no podían pasar de peones. Había también gitanos, esquiladores de mulas y de perros, y no faltaban cargadores, barberos ambulantes y saltimbanquis. Casi todos ellos, si se terciaba, robaban lo que podían; todos presentaban el mismo aspecto de miseria y de consunción. Todos sentían una rabia constante, que se manifestaba en imprecaciones furiosas y en blasfemias. (p. 288)[18]

Characteristically, amidst debasing animal associations ('como una gusanera', 'como un reptil [cambia] de piel'), analysis and synthesis interact: on the one hand, the repeated listing of varied trades and activities — and half activities and non-activities —, with significant climaxes at 'se moría de hambre', 'se prostituían mujeres' and 'medio ladrones'; on the other hand, the gathering together of common characteristics ('Casi todos ellos...; todos presentaban.... Todos sentían...', with an effective progression

---

[18] The description has been much developed in the transition from the *El Globo* version. The first paragraph, it will be noted, was completely absent in 1903:

> No llegó á conocer Manuel á todos, sino á muy pocos de los vecinos de la casa; se decía que puestos en fila los que allí habitaban llegarían desde el Arroyo de Embajadores hasta la plaza del Progreso.
>
> Era, en general, aquella gente, gente descentrada, que vivía en un continuo aplanamiento producido por su eterna miseria; muchos cambiaban de oficio como un reptil puede cambiar de piel; la mayoría eran peones de carpintero y de albañil, que p[r]obablemente no lograron aprender en su vida más que á serrar ó á amasar yeso; había también gitanos, esquiladores de mulas y de perros, y no faltaban cargadores, barberos ambulantes y salti[m]banquis. Casi todos ellos, si se terciaba, robaban lo que podían; todos presentaban el mismo carácter de miseria y de consunción. (*El Globo*, 13 March 1903)

from one of the climactic activities, 'robaban', to 'el mismo aspecto' and on to the same reaction of anger), emphasis on the all-enveloping 'miseria' and pointers to causes and consequences ('producido por...', 'a consecuencia de...', 'Todos sentían...') — in short, both emphasis on observed reality and probing of its significance. Both in the vividness and immediacy of expression and in the way in which observation and significance are interwoven it is very different from the sort of thing that we find most commonly in contemporary press and official reports with their usually brief, generic and anaemic references to 'desgraciados' (a favourite word), 'infelices', 'indigentes', 'gentes necesitadas', 'clases menesterosas', etc.

Manuel finds even more degrading conditions in his wanderings with the Piratas down by the Arroyo de Embajadores — where the 'delegado municipal de cementerios', in 1888, drew attention to 'los albergues sucios y nocivos' and the consequently high death rate (Puértolas, p. 43) —: first in the Casa del Cabrero, 'un grupo de casuchas bajas con un patio estrecho y largo en medio' where mothers and daughters alike are mostly prostitutes and the children seem to sense 'la degradación de su miseria' (p. 284); then along the edge of the Manzanares, at the far end of the Dehesa de la Arganzuela, where the council did in fact keep its refuse-disposal equipment (*El Globo*, 15 January 1899; cf. *LB*, p. 285) and where Manuel sees 'barracas de esteras sucias y mugrientas: chozas de aduar africano, construidas sobre armazón de palitroques y cañas' (p. 285).

In Part III of *La busca* we learn of still more primitive living conditions: the 'cuchitril formado por cuatro esteras en el lavadero del Manzanares' where an eighty-year-old man slept, and died of cold when *golfos* pulled his matting back (p. 337), the cave where El Cojo lives, 'un agujero hecho en la arena' (p. 337), the caves of La Montaña where a group of *golfos* sleep, so nightmarish to Manuel that he prefers to freeze outside (p. 355). This last point is possibly significant, as indeed, perhaps, is the generally reduced immediacy and vividness in the portrayal of living conditions after the Corralón. One suspects that here were conditions that Baroja, ever dependent for his descriptions on 'la impresión directa', had observed less closely and therefore felt less able to describe. With the Corralón as our yardstick of degradation we are given to understand — and we accept — that subsequent conditions are worse; nevertheless we are not always made to feel this. In the last example referred to, the 'vaho pestilente' that emanates from the cave, the shadowy figures within and Manuel's 'pensó haber visto algo parecido en la pesadilla de una fiebre' are uncharacteristically thin; his decision to sleep outside is conceivably a pointer to authorial evasiveness.

Not everyone in *La busca* has a regular sleeping-place, however primitive, and Manuel himself sleeps on occasion in the doorway of the Observatory (p. 337), on benches in the Plaza de Oriente and on seats in the Castellana (p. 354). El Expósito is the clearest example of this rootless, nomadic existence:

—Y tú ¿no has tenido nunca casa?

—Yo no.

—¿Y dónde sueles dormir?

—Pues, en el verano, en las cuevas y en los corrales, y en el invierno, en las calderas del asfalto.

—¿Y cuando no hay asfalto?

—En algún asilo. (p. 335)

The Madrid press of the period carried daily reports of the number of people lodged in the various hostels of the city and Puértolas and Moral both quote examples. In 1899, in a survey of the most notable social problems of the capital, the Governor of Madrid included a reference to the problem of the homeless: 'más de mil indigentes de ambos sexos y de todas las edades, que no tienen casa ni hogar, duermen todas las noches en los Asilos municipales, en el Refugio y en las Casas de Socorro y en las delegaciones de Vigilancia de los diez distritos de la capital' (*El Globo*, 29 January 1899). If the 'asilo' was only the last resort for many, as it was for El Expósito, this report of the Governor, like the daily press reports, hardly expresses the full gravity of the problem. On the last night of the novel we find Manuel himself, amidst 'grupos de hombres y de chiquillos astrosos', huddled around the pitch cauldrons in the Puerta del Sol (p. 371).

I turn now from living conditions to human activity. We have seen a profusion of pointers in the description of the Corralón. There is further evidence elsewhere in the novel. I start with the world of work. It plays only a small part in *La busca* — as also in Baroja's other novels — and it is significant that Puértolas and Moral, in the corresponding sections of their studies (Puértolas, pp. 88-97; Moral, pp. 155-76), devote their main energies to supplementing Baroja's evidence with material drawn from other sources and refer to *La busca* only with reference to III,ɪ: the bakery, referred to by both Puértolas and Moral and Tío Patas' shop, referred to by Puértolas. In Moral's own words, 'como Baroja sólo nos habla y proporciona datos de ciertos oficios y aspectos, enriqueceremos las aportaciones barojianas con otros testimonios tomados de fuentes de la época' (p. 155). This, I repeat, is significant and we shall return to the point. For the moment, however, it can be observed that the world of work does in fact appear rather more frequently than this, but rarely at the focus of attention. Thus, we see La Petra, weary after her day's work as a boarding-house servant, but attention is quickly diverted to immoral goings-on across the street (p. 258); similarly, brief later references to her work yield immediately either to the 'complot' and 'bromas' of the guests or to the strikingly unappetizing meal being prepared or to La Petra's preoccupations about her son Manuel (pp. 262-5). Similarly again, in Tío Patas' shop, Manuel had to work hard all morning, we are told, but the emphasis is on the — for him — far more irksome need to sit still in the afternoon, 'detrás del mostrador, aburriéndose, vigilado por el ama y su cuñada', and on the subsequent 'historia [...] verdaderamente interesante' of Tío Patas (pp. 325-6). In the presentation of both these aspects of work, then, Baroja characteristically diverts the reader's attention from the work itself to other things: to Manuel's situation and to picturesque episodes. In three cases in *La busca*, however, there is greater emphasis on work: in the *zapatería*, in the bakery and at Señor Custodio's. I review them briefly in turn.

'El señor Ignacio, maestro de obra prima, había tenido

necesidad por falta de trabajo, de abandonar la lezna y el tirapié para dedicarse a las tenazas y a la cuchilla; de crear, a destruir; de hacer botas nuevas, a destripar botas viejas' (p. 280). The emphasis, then, is less on work than on the absence of work and one is reminded that Madrid at the end of the nineteenth century was still very much a city of artisans, but in a context of economic recession (Moral, pp. 27-39). Certainly there seems to be a parallel between Ignacio's neighbour and rival, 'que sólo de Pascuas a Ramos tenía alguna mala chapuza que hacer' (p. 280), and tailors' assistants who at certain times of the year, were fortunate to have work for four days a week (Moral, p. 156). Baroja's cobblers, however, are in an even worse position and his description serves as a starting-point for ironic references to the state of Spain itself. It also serves to emphasize another area of *sujeción* for Manuel.

The description of Manuel's two months as a baker's apprentice is clearly based on the author's own experience when he was in joint charge of his aunt's bakery from 1896 to 1902. The outline of the apprentice's day, says Moral, is described 'minuciosamente': a fifteen-to-seventeen-hour day, for which he was paid 'siete reales' (pp. 172-3; cf. *LB*, p. 327). 'Igualmente duro', she continues, 'era el trabajo para los oficiales que para el aprendiz.' She does well to make the point, for Baroja does not, and there is a significant difference between 'describe minuciosamente', which she rightly applies to Manuel's work, and her inference of equally hard work by his Galician superiors. However justified the inference may be from a real-life point of view, Baroja does not make us feel this. We see life very much from Manuel's standpoint, and from his standpoint the Galicians, with their insensitivity and their bullying, are more oppressors than oppressed. As in Tío Patas' shop Baroja has sacrificed an element of work oppression to bring out Manuel's own particular situation — *sujeción* at Tío Patas'; lack of affection in the bakery — and the potential class significance of work in the bakery has clearly been sacrificed to a purely individual response. It is an important point and I shall return to it. In her ensuing pages Moral reminds us that Baroja's description of the bakehouse itself, in a 'sótano oscuro, triste y sucio' (*LB*, pp. 326-7), and his reference to a 'viejo, mozo de la tahona, enfermo de catarro crónico por la infiltración de harina en el pulmón' (*LB*, p. 327) were both firmly rooted in reality.

I turn finally to the world of work of Señor Custodio, the refuse-collector. The description of his donkey cart, 'compuesto de tiras de pleita, con su chapa y su número' and with its 'sacos, cubos y espuertas' — even to the dog running along underneath — (p. 356) will evoke memories for anyone who knew Madrid even as late as the 1950s, though the carts that I myself recall were pulled by mules rather than donkeys. Equally realistic is the description of the *trapero*'s daily round and his subsequent sorting and disposal of the materials collected (pp. 359-60). Indeed, in the light of Custodio's subsequent calculations of the potential wealth to be made from 'toda la basura que sale de Madrid' (p. 361) one wonders if Baroja here recalled a submission made in 1899 by a certain Don Juan Guillén Palomar to the Mayor of Madrid in which he asked for an exclusive twenty-five-year concession entitling him to collect and dispose of 'las basuras, detritus, desperdicios, alimentos averiados, animales para destruir y muertos de la vía pública, Mataderos, Mercados, y edificios de su propiedad [etc.]', a concession, he claimed, that would serve both to improve the cleanliness of the city and to provide fertilizers for the land (*El Globo*, 15 January 1899). To this end he further asked for the lease of the 'sitio denominado Pradera del Canal, dehesa de la Arganzuela', which Baroja, also in *La busca*, describes with its 'carros de riego, barredoras mecánicas, bombas de extraer pozos negros, montones de escobas y otra porción de menesteres y utensilios de la limpieza urbana' (p. 285).

At a lower level than Ignacio, the bakers and Custodio are the itinerant hawkers and pedlars and street entertainers who are glimpsed at various moments in the novel: the four blind residents of the Corralón, for example, 'los cuales [...] tocaban por las calles los últimos tangos, tientos y coplas de zarzuela' (p. 289); even Don Alonso, who has fallen on bad times and now has to hawk El Tabuenca's various contraptions round bars and cafés. From this world it is but a short distance to that of the beggar. 'La mendicidad', declared the Governor of Madrid in 1899, 'a pesar de todos los esfuerzos hechos para evitarla ó reprimirla, crece por momentos; cuatro mil desgraciados acuden diariamente al Comedor de Caridad' (*El Globo*, 29 January 1899). Baroja describes such 'desgraciados' repeatedly in *La busca*; he also shows them queuing up for food at the María Cristina barracks, near Atocha station (p. 336). But the fullest and finest description of them is at another charitable institution, the Doctrina, where beneficent and pious ladies seek to impart religious instruction to beggars attracted by the possibility of more readily convertible offerings. I have no specific information on the Doctrina, 'por el camino alto de San Isidro'; I have, however, noted a press announcement of a comparable dispensing of charity:

> Para completar la obra [de caridad de la Casa de Socorro de Palacio] hoy día de Reyes, á las once de la mañana, se hará el reparto de ropas nuevas á los desgraciados del distrito que lo han solicitado, siendo el número de éstas el de 150 mantas, 200 sábanas, 50 jergones, 50 mantones, 80 camisetas de abrigo, 12 bufandas, 24 pares de calzoncillos, 50 chalecos de Bayona y 32 envolturas. (*El Globo*, 6 January 1899)

'Personas caritativas' were further beseeched to 'honr[ar] con su presencia este acto, como igualmente asistan á la cena que se da diariamente á los albergados á las siete de la tarde'. The said 'personas caritativas' would surely have been shocked by the comments of Baroja's beggars (pp. 293-4); nor, one imagines, would they have greatly relished the appearance of the beggars themselves:

> no se veían más que caras hinchadas, de estúpida apariencia, narices inflamadas y bocas torcidas; viejas gordas y pesadas como ballenas melancólicas; viejezuelas esqueléticas de boca hundida y nariz de ave rapaz; mendigas vergonzantes con la barba verrugosa, llena de pelos, y la mirada entre irónica y huraña; mujeres jóvenes, flacas y extenuadas, desmelenadas y negras; y todas, viejas y jóvenes, envueltas en trajes raídos, remendados, zurcidos y vueltos a remendar hasta no dejar

una pulgada sin su remiendo. Los mantones verdes, de color
de aceituna, y el traje triste ciudadano alternaban con los
refajos de bayeta, amarillos y rojos, de las campesinas. (p.
291)[19]

It is a good example of Baroja's descriptive technique and it
should perhaps prompt us to question the traditional emphasis
on his mere realism — and even his self-declared impressionism.
One can note, first, the emphasis on perception and the
subsequent listing, all dependent, up to 'sin su remiendo', on the
single verb 'veían', with no weakening 'había' (as there was in
the 1903 version: 'había viejas gordas y pesadas'). But the
starting-point is an all-embracing 'no se veían más que caras
hinchadas, de estúpida apariencia' which thereby becomes an
attribute of the whole scene (as opposed to the 1903 non-
exclusive survey, 'Por todas partes se veían...'). Thereafter one
notes: the clinical eye for physical and psychological ugliness
and deformity and degeneration; the debasing animal imagery
('ballenas' and 'ave rapaz' are both absent from the 1903
version); the interweaving of contrasts (analysis) and similarities
(synthesis): contrasts in what Baroja sees as subordinate (fat-
thin, young-old, town-country) and similarities in what he sees
as significant and revealing (the 'caras hinchadas [etc.]' at the
beginning: the 'trajes raídos' near the end); thereafter, the
emphasis on specific details of *lo raído* (all very different from
the 1903 version which, from here to the end of the paragraph,
had the women less sombrely 'envueltas en harapos pintorescos,
refajos de bayeta de distintos colores llenos de remiendos');
finally, the emotional diminuendo of the last sentence, realistic,
impressionistic, the starting-point from which a less expression-
istic description of the Corte de los Milagros might well have
taken its starting-point.

[19] Entraron la señora Jacoba y los dos chicos en el patio. Parecía aquello una
reunión de mendigos en su Corte de los Milagros. Por todas partes se veían
caras hinchadas de estúpida apariencia, ojos rojos y sin pestañas, narices
inflamadas, bocas torcidas; había viejas gordas y pesadas, viejezuelas de
nariz como un pico, barba puntiaguda y boca hundida; mujeres flacas, de
color de tierra; todas, viejas y jóvenes, envueltas en harapos pintorescos,
refajos de bayeta de distintos colores llenos de remiendos. (*El Globo*, 15
March 1903)

From beggars one passes easily to *golfos* and others who operate on the fringes of the law and beyond. As evidence that Baroja saw the *golfo* as a real-life problem one can point to two articles that appeared before *La busca*: 'Patología del golfo' (1899; V, 55-9), published under his title 'doctor Baroja' and with corresponding medical terminology, and 'Mala hierba' (1902; V, 41-2). As evidence that others, too, saw the *golfos* as a problem one can consult Luis Maristany's well-documented study of those articles (*22*), which serves nicely to supplement the evidence adduced by Puértolas and Moral. For Baroja *golfería* was a phenomenon found at all levels of society: from the 'hampa o golfería miserable que se refugia en los barrios pobres, como las Injurias, las Cambroneras [etc.]' to the 'golfería aristocrática, formada por señores muy finos' (V, 41-2). In *La busca*, however, we are concerned only with *golfería* at the lowest social level: 'La componen los que viven de la busca, pidiendo limosna, *mangando* lo que se tenía [*sic also in 1902, but perhaps read* se tercia]; forma este hampa el mundo de los randas, mangantes, descuideros, ninchis, golfos propiamente dichos, como diría cualquier profesor de los nuestros, y golfolaires' (V, 41). Some, like El Expósito, have no family and it is significant that Baroja, with his compassion for anyone truly trodden down by circumstances, presents him in a favourable light: with no evidence of criminality, sharing his bread with Manuel, taking him to the María Cristina barracks, and merely indulging in a little harmless 'guasa' at the expense of a Catalan quack and his 'costilla' (pp. 335-6). As for his occupations, '—¡Psch!..., lo que se tercia: cojo colillas, vendo arena, y cuando no gano nada voy al cuartel de María Cristina' (p. 335). Others, like Vidal and El Bizco, have families, but break away from them at an early age: Vidal goes off 'golfeando y sin querer trabajar' (p. 330); El Bizco, 'un bruto, una alimaña digna de exterminio', after regularly robbing his father, 'un miserable tejedor de caña' — with our emotions thus brought clearly to bear against him — proceeds to extend the range of his 'brutalidad y animalidad repelentes' (p. 296). They, too, live 'A lo que cae' (p. 331), but '¡Trabajar!... *Pa* el gato' (p. 332).

Shortly afterwards Manuel meets more *golfos* and is shocked by
their vicious 'mala intención' as they spend the night together
sheltering in the portico of the Observatory (p. 337). El
Expósito's *golfería*, it will be noted, is interposed between that
of El Bizco and Vidal and that of the boys in the Observatory.
This fact, together with the notable difference of treatment —
sympathetic in the first case; hostile in the other two —, does not
suggest the 'fría objetividad' or 'frialdad sardónica' that Baroja
has been accused of (VII, 483). Nor does it suggest 'la
observación de una máquina inerte e indiferente' that Navarro
Ledesma found in *La busca*. 'Creo que Navarro Ledesma se
engañaba,' commented Baroja in his typically low key (VII,
753). One need be less low-key in one's agreement with him.

Some *golfos*, said Baroja in his 1902 article, become 'personas
decentes', others become 'pinchos, ganchos o rateros' — like El
Pastiri, for instance, with his sleight of hand (pp. 316, 345-6),
examples of both of which can still be seen in the Rastro,
complete with 'ganchos', on any Sunday —; yet others are
'notables equilibristas que se pasan toda la vida en equilibrio
inestable, pero sin caerse' (V, 58). These are the possibilities
open to Manuel, for he too is a *golfo* and he shares the *golfos*'
'instintos aventureros' and their impatience with 'sujeción'. But
not their amorality, much less the positive viciousness and 'mala
intención' that is evident in most of them. Here as elsewhere
Manuel is the generally impassive but basically moral guide to
the world of *La busca*. Baroja, as we have seen, no less moral, is
rather less impassive. We shall return to the point in a later
chapter.

Vidal's and Manuel's transfer of activity from petty crime in
the outskirts to Apolo claque and prostitute protection in the
centre extends the range of their typically *golfo* activities (cf. V,
57) and brings them into contact with the other obvious area of
'la busca': alongside the *golfos*, the prostitutes. In fact, we
glimpsed something of their world both in and from Doña
Casiana's boarding-house — on the one hand, the near
amateurs, Celia and Irene, within the boarding-house; on the
other hand, the full-fledged professionals across the street —

and there have been further pointers to prostitution: in the
Corralón, in the Casa del Cabrero, in La Blasa's tavern, in the
streets of Madrid.... With the appearance of La Mellá, La Goya,
La Rabanitos and La Engracia the world of the prostitute takes
its turn at the focus of attention (pp. 352-4). But as in his
presentation of other aspects of low life Baroja deals not in
abstractions or statistics or anaemic generic expressions. He is
concerned with vividly portrayed individuals. La Mellá, the
ugliest of the four, 'con su cabeza gorda y disforme, los ojos
negros, la boca grande con los dientes rotos, el cuerpo
rechoncho, parecía la bufona de una antigua princesa', but she
was 'siempre alegre, a todas horas cantando y riendo' — a
reminder of the vitality that Baroja finds even in degradation
and that commentators commonly overlook. La Goya, 'como
más bonita', is significantly not described; Baroja concentrates
instead on the exploitation of her by her protector, El Soldadito
— a fine example of the author's selective vision, with the brief
reference to La Goya's prettiness used primarily as a yardstick
by which to emphasize her protector's bestiality.[20] La Rabanitos
'parecía una mujer en miniatura: una carita blanca con manchas
azules alrededor de la nariz y de la boca; un cuerpecillo raquítico
y delgaducho; una vieja, con su mantoncito oscuro y su falda
negra [...]. Echaba sangre por la boca con frecuencia'. La
Engracia, the last of the four, is the most fully described and, as
'el tipo de la mujer de burdel', is seen as the most representative:
'Llevaba ocho años de buscona y tenía diecisiete. Se lamentaba
de haber crecido, porque decía que de niña ganaba más'. She is
also presented as the most bestial of the four (among prostitutes
as among other humans, it seems, the most typical for Baroja is
also the most bestial). The 1903 version of her portrait follows
for comparison.[21]

[20] Compare the treatment of Salomé, referred to in Chapter 3. Again and again
in Baroja it is relevant to ask oneself, in the words of an early commentator,
'¿Contra quién va dirigido ese elogio?'

[21] La Engracia, la otra favorita de Vidal, á pesar de que no tenía más de
catorce ó quince años, era el tipo de la mujer de burdel; la cara blanca por los
polvos de arroz, los ojos brillantes; á veces su cara tenía una expresión de
melancolía puramente animal; al sonreir enseñaba los dientes, azulados, que

contrastaban con la blancura de la cara empolvada, y su sonrisa era una mezcla de estupidez y de alegría canalla, que sorprendía.

El tono de su risa era también ambiguo y falso. Solía vestir blusas vistosas, azules y rojas, pañuelo blanco en la cabeza y delantal de color, y andaba siempre corriendo de un lado á otro, haciendo sonar las monedas que llevaba en el bolsillo.

La Engracia hablaba poco, y cuando hablaba era para decir algo muy bestial y muy sucio, lo que le producía una gran alegría. (*El Globo*, 28-9 March 1903)

6. Baroja and social awareness

Faced with the squalid conditions and human degradation indicated in the previous chapter it is tempting for the socially conscious reader of today to find in *La busca* an intentional laying bare of social evils — perhaps even to see it as a novel of social protest — and to emphasize the trilogy to which it belongs as a progression towards political awareness. The most notable study in this direction is by Carlos Blanco Aguinaga (*29*). But Blanco Aguinaga knows too well Baroja's declared antipathy to democracy and socialism and *regeneración* — and indeed his whole 'mentalidad antisocial' and 'antiprogresista' (p. 230) — to believe that the novelist was aiming to reform the society he described. What he does find, however, is 'un gran conocimiento de la realidad social de su tiempo, una penetrante capacidad de observación objetiva' (p. 230), and he believes that Baroja's 'extraordinario realismo objetivo' as a novelist came into conflict with his repeatedly declared ideological standpoint as a petit bourgeois. In other words, if I interpret Blanco Aguinaga correctly, Baroja could not be aware of so much misery and degradation and still, without 'escamateo ideológico' (p. 230), maintain a bourgeois standpoint.

The influence of Blanco Aguinaga's study on other scholars (Puértolas, Moral, Carenas, Neuschäfer...), plus the fact that it typifies an approach now common in Spanish literary studies, makes it necessary to consider the work closely. Because of its length and copious argument it is impossible in a few pages to do justice either to the study or to one's objections to it. Its importance, however, obliges one to try. Taken in isolation from Baroja's trilogy it reads convincingly and the arguments hold together well. Unfortunately, the relationship of the study to Baroja's trilogy is not notably close. Selection, supplementation and subjective highlighting seem to play as great a part in Blanco Aguinaga's study as they do in Baroja's novels. The direction in which they take us, however, is very different.

Manuel, according to Blanco Aguinaga, typifies the immigrant worker of his day, driven by poverty from the land and drifting into Madrid where, because of the lack of industry and the excess of bureaucracy, the immigrant's only choice seemed to lie between service within the city and *golfería* on the outskirts. The Estación del Mediodía, Atocha station, where Manuel arrives, is significantly on the borderline between these two Madrids. Because of his mother's 'privileged' position Manuel is able to start with service within the city and he spends his first weeks working in Doña Casiana's boarding-house. But it is a false start. He develops the traditional *pícaro*'s attitudes and his move downhill begins. Blanco Aguinaga makes much of this move downhill, for the poor quarter to the south, to which Manuel is transferred, lies topographically at a lower level than the centre of Madrid. It is therefore, in a real as well as a metaphorical sense, a move downhill. And not only downhill, but also outwards, from the more prosperous area of the centre to the poverty of the outskirts. The centre of Madrid, says Blanco Aguinaga, is depicted as a citadel, a well defended enemy fortress that those below must conquer. And dominating the citadel, as one looks upwards from the poor quarter below, are those three elements of oppression: the Church (symbolized by the Church of the Almudena), the Nobility (symbolized by the Royal Palace) and the Army (symbolized by the Montaña barracks). It is all very different from the more attractive views that the more prosperous inhabitants of the centre enjoy: out over the countryside, beyond 'la enorme desolación de los alrededores madrileños' (*MH*, p. 457), to where there are plains with 'suaves ondulaciones' and the Manzanares is 'como un hilo de plata', or northwestwards towards the Guadarrama 'con las crestas blanqueadas por la nieve' (*LB*, p. 338). Blanco Aguinaga will make his main point again and again: '*La lucha por la vida* gira alrededor de las muy precisas relaciones topográfico-sociales "dentro-fuera", "arriba-abajo"' (p. 239); 'la estructura real de la trilogía, que es, insistamos en ello, sociológica y geográfica' (p. 245); 'Evidente es el rigor formal de esta obra de Baroja, cuyos dos ejes principales, el sociológico y el topográfico, le dan unidad y sentido' (p. 249).... And always with the notion of oppression and class conflict close at hand: contrasts between 'los de abajo' and 'los de arriba' (p. 237); a 'ciudadela a conquistar' (p. 237); 'el reducto enemigo' (p. 239); 'Bajo mundo [...], enemigo de las tan pregonadas virtudes burguesas del XIX' (p. 240)....

But meanwhile the critic has gone on to survey, in ascending social order, the different types of people who live in these deprived areas: men and women cast out by urban life ('ex faranduleros, golfos agotados, ex prostitutas; viejos ya todos', p. 238); *golfos* (a minority of 'salvajes', like El Bizco, who will never get into the city and others, like Vidal, who want to and do, pp. 238-9); 'cierto tipo de gente de trabajo [...], cuyos oficios limitaremos — para simplificar, y porque así lo hace Baroja — al del trapero, señor Custodio', who lives off the city but has no desire to live there (pp. 241-2); workers ('correctores de pruebas, albañiles, obreros de la compañía de gas', 'los verdaderos asaltantes de la alta ciudadela del simbólico Cuartel de la Montaña', 'críticos feroces del sistema' (evidence of all this is notably lacking in Blanco Aguinaga's survey — and in *La busca*), though they are 'criticados duramente por los "honrados" trabajadores serios sin conciencia de clase' (who, presumably because of this last characteristic, are not included and examined by Blanco Aguinaga in their own right, pp. 242-4).

In the final and longest part of his study Blanco Aguinaga follows Manuel step by step through the trilogy. Here I shall confine my survey to the pages on *La busca*. From Doña Casiana's boarding-house Manuel starts on his downhill progress and proceeds by stages that are 'perfectamente precisadas en términos de la topografía de la zona Sur de Madrid' (p. 246). Thus, he is escorted first, downhill, to the *zapatería* and on the following Sunday he is taken to Ignacio's house, 'una casa pobre [...] a caballo todavía entre la respetabilidad y la degradación' (p. 249). But then he goes off

with Vidal to meet El Bizco and his gang and they go down
further: 'Bajan todos al arroyo de Embajadores y llegan "a una
barriada miserable y pequeña"'. 'Por ahí se encontraba el
"Corralón" [...], vivienda de cientos, con patios, traspatios,
galerías, suciedad, enfermedades y trastos inservibles. "Cada
trozo de galería era manifestación de una vida distinta dentro del
comunismo del hambre [...]"' (p. 250). This 'barriada recién
descubierta' frightens Manuel and they leave.[22] Subsequently he
himself goes to live there and thereafter, during a large part of
the rest of the novel he will live the 'agobiante vida doble del
obrero apicarado' (pp. 251-2). When his cousin dies and Ignacio
falls ill Manuel goes to work in a greengrocer's and, afterwards,
in a bakery. 'Al mismo tiempo, acostumbrado ya a las barriadas
miserables, se dedica a corretear por las afueras. "Vidal y él se
escapaban de casa [cada cual de la suya] con cualquier pretexto
[...]". En la insoportable tensión entre las dos vidas, la de
dentro y la de fuera de la ciudad, vence, por fin, la golfería: deja
un día Manuel de trabajar [etc.].'[23] He leaves this life by

[22] I am trying to confine myself in these initial pages to exposition and to
withold comments until later. However, Blanco Aguinaga has here erred on a
specific point. It is Ignacio who lives in the Corralón where 'cada galería era
manifestación de una vida distinta dentro del comunismo del hambre' (cf.
'En el espacio [del Corralón] que disfrutaba la familia del zapatero', *LB*, p.
287; 'Si quiere ver la señora la casa donde vivimos nosotros, es éste—dijo
Leandro. Pasaron al interior del Corralón' p. 299). The *barriada* below is the
Casa del Cabrero. Blanco Aguinaga mistakenly brings them together.
   The mistake itself scarcely matters. What is worrying — and already
indicative of the fallaciousness of Blanco Aguinaga's topographical evidence
— is that he finds Ignacio's house poor but 'a caballo todavía entre la
respetabilidad y la degradación', yet asssociates the squalor of the Corralón
(which he has failed to notice is the same building) with a lower topographical
level. 'Etapas perfectamente precisadas en términos de la topografía'? Or
underlying determination by the critic to make a case conceived *a priori*?
Here as elsewhere Baroja is showing different human responses to the general
misery of the Corralón: cf. 'Aquí se advertía cierta limpieza y curiosidad
[...]; allá se traslucía cierto instinto utilitario [...]. Pero, en general, no se
veían más que ropas sucias [...]' (*LB*, p. 287). Blanco Aguinaga, with his
exaggerated left-wing tendency to see man as a slave of physical conditions,
allows for no such differences.

[23] Apart from some misleading chronological references — the *escapadas* do
not coincide with Manuel's period of work 'dentro de la ciudad' and he

accident when he is picked up by Señor Custodio, but finally
leaves Custodio's house because of 'una decepción amorosa'
and finishes up in the Puerta del Sol huddled together with
'pícaros, mendigos y golfos [que] *parecen* posesionarse
simbólica y momentáneamente de lo anhelado — la ciudad —,
en tanto que Manuel, que ha llegado con todos ellos, acaba por
separarse mentalmente del mundo que así, como en andas, le ha
traído hasta el centro mismo [...]. Centro de la vida moderna, la
ciudad atrae a todos y, quiéranlo o no sus respetables y
sorprendidos habitantes, tiene la obligación de absorber a todos
los que a ella acuden' (pp. 253-4).

In the rest of his study Blanco Aguinaga follows Manuel's
adventures in similar fashion through *Mala hierba* and *Aurora
roja* and concludes with expressions of disappointment about
the last novel in the trilogy in which he finds 'una profunda
falsificación de las posibilidades abiertas en las dos primeras
partes de la trilogía' (p. 281). Certainly, he admits, the novelist is
the god of his own creation. Nevertheless, he continues, 'la
realidad objetiva de la obra misma puede—y debe—imponerse a
cualquier arbitrariedad del Dios que *no* es omnipotente' (p.
281), instead of which Baroja imposes 'su propia visión sujetiva
del mundo' (p. 286), attributing Spanish ills not to social
conditions but to innate Spanish character: 'la indiferencia por
el trabajo' and the lack of 'el sentimiento del valor, de la
dignidad y de la gratitud' (*AR*, p. 551) — 'vulgares tópicos'
according to Blanco Aguinaga —, and thus advocating the need
for enlightened despotism. Despite this, concludes Blanco
Aguinaga, in *La lucha por la vida* 'Baroja llegó a ver la realidad
española de fin de siglo desde una perspectiva sólo posible
(entonces) a partir de ciertos postulados sobre la lucha de clases
característicos del pensamiento revolucionario' (p. 290).

> leaves his job not because *golfería* prevails after 'tensión entre las dos vidas'
> but because he falls ill — Blanco Aguinaga continues with his mistaken belief
> that Manuel, whilst working in the cobbler's shop, lives in a different house
> from Vidal, '[cada cual de la suya]', whereas in fact he clearly lives with his
> cousin's family: cf. 'Algunas noches Manuel oía a Leandro en su cuarto que
> se revolvía en la cama y suspiraba' (*LB*, p. 313) and Leandra's 'aquí yo no te
> puedo tener' when Manuel has to leave (*LB*, p. 324), together with much
> more indisputable evidence.

* * * * * *

   The severity of Blanco Aguinaga's criticisms of Baroja makes
it somewhat easier to express one's objections to the critic's own
study. 'Escamoteo ideológico' (p. 230)? 'Profunda falsificación'
(p. 281)? 'Va recargando las tintas que convienen a su particular
visión *política* del mundo' (p. 282)? 'Sujetivismo' (p. 286)? 'En
pleno delirio de sus muy personales mitomanías' (p. 289)? 'Deja
de jugar limpio' (p. 289)? Baroja perhaps; Carlos Blanco
Aguinaga certainly. And the novelist, being the god of his own
creation, has the right to interpret as he will; the critic, on the
other hand, as a mere servant of literature, has not.
   We can pass quickly, for the moment, over Blanco
Aguinaga's insistence on the duality of 'objective realism' (the
harsh conditions that Baroja sees and portrays) and
'subjectivism' (the unsatisfactory solution and commentary that
Baroja offers) and come immediately to his closer survey of the
novel. Does Manuel really typify the immigrant worker, driven
by poverty from the land (most notably in Andalusia, p. 237)? If
so, Baroja has not made a very good case: in the first place,
Manuel was apparently born in Madrid and he lived there until
two years before the novel opens; in the second place, he did not
come from Andalusia in the south but from Soria in the north;
finally and especially, he came to Madrid not because of poor
working conditions but because his mother was there and
because he found life with his relatives unpleasant: they showed
him no affection, the village where they lived was in the middle
of nowhere, he did not want to study and he had a sense of
adventure. In other words, he came to Madrid for reasons of
personal circumstance and psychology, not because of economic
or social conditions. Similarly, Blanco Aguinaga is misleadingly
selective when he says of La Petra simply 'de mujer de obrero ha
pasado a sirvienta sin hogar propio' (p. 232), as though she had
been driven to this by the inevitable hardships of widowhood.
When her husband died, Petra had her own boarding-house with
reliable guests who advised her to stay on, but because she
disliked that part of Madrid (and presumably also because she

was notably 'voluntariosa' and 'de una testarudez de mula', *LB*, p. 263) — psychological reasons again — she moved elsewhere, took in 'gente informal y sin dinero, que dejaban a deber mucho' (p. 263) and was finally driven into debt and on to Doña Casiana's. And where are the economic and social causes of Manuel's move downhill from the centre? So far as one can see, he moved downhill simply because he came to blows with one of the lodgers. And what justification is there for Blanco Aguinaga's emphasis on the geographical situation of the railway station where Manuel arrives, on the frontier between the two Madrids, or on the downhill movement towards the poor quarter, or on Madrid as a fortress to be stormed by those below? I find no evidence that Baroja himself emphasizes any of these things. We are not concerned with a symbolic Kafkaesque world in which the author creates his own topography. We are concerned with Madrid as it was. Blanco Aguinaga may find special significance in the situation of the station but it is difficult to see that Baroja did. He seems simply to have accepted it as the obvious place where Manuel would arrive in Madrid.[24] Similarly, it is true that Manuel's move from the centre of the capital represents both a literal and a metaphorical move downhill, but I do not find that Baroja stresses either of these things. On the contrary, Manuel finds that the 'hermosa casa' where he sleeps on the first night, in the Calle del Aguila, is 'bastante mejor que la de la casa de huéspedes' and he falls asleep 'Pes[ando] el pro y contra de su nueva posición social y calculando si el fiel de la balanza se inclinaría a uno u otro lado' (*LB*, p. 282). Moreover, once he is settled there, 'aquellas barriadas miserables [around the Corralón] se le antojaban llenas de atractivos' (p. 295). Besides, despite the inverted commas round "cuesta abajo", the starting-point of Blanco Aguinaga's lucubrations on the subject (p. 234), the expression is not Baroja's but the critic's own, and we have already seen the singularly elastic use that Blanco Aguinaga makes of Baroja's

[24] The Soria train (with change at Alcuneza) reached the Estación del Mediodía daily at 9.50 p.m. (*Almanaque y guía matritense: año 1896*, Madrid [1895], p. 92).

evidence and the way in which he is able to adapt that evidence
even to his own topographical misinterpretation of the novel
(above, p. 76 n.). Finally, the worst living conditions depicted in
La busca — so bad that they seemed to Manuel like something
out of a feverish nightmare — are unfortunately omitted by
Blanco Aguinaga from his survey: they are the Cuevas de la
Montaña del Príncipe Pío, 'montes más altos que veinte casas de
éstas' (p. 281); to get to them Manuel and El Bizco 'subieron por
una vereda estrecha' (p. 355).

One could continue in like manner through Blanco
Aguinaga's study. However, among the above observations I
have touched on two points to which the critic gives special
importance and emphasis: alleged topographical significance
and alleged panoramas of oppression, both of which encourage
him to see the novel in terms of class conflict. I shall concentrate
henceforth on these points.

Firstly, alleged topographical significance. In *La busca* there
are two main passages in which Baroja surveys the areas of
activity of El Bizco and of other *golfos* and *randas*. They are the
following:

Se conocían, por lo que decía Vidal, todos los randas, hasta
los de los barrios más lejanos. Era una vida extrasocial la
suya, admirable; hoy se veían en los Cuatro Caminos, a los
tres o cuatro días en el puente de Vallecas o en la Guindalera;
se ayudaban unos a otros.

Su radio de acción era una zona comprendida desde el
extremo de la Casa de Campo, en donde se encuentran el
ventorro de Agapito y las ventas de Alcorcón, hasta los
Carabancheles; desde aquí, las orillas del arroyo Abroñigal,
la Elipa, el Este, las Ventas y la Concepción hasta la
Prosperidad; luego, Tetuán hasta la Puerta de Hierro.
Dormían, en verano, en corrales y cobertizos de las afueras.

Los del centro, mejor vestidos, más aristócratas, tenían ya
su golfa, a la que fiscalizaban las ganancias y que se cuidaban
de ellos; pero la golfería del centro era ya distinta, de otra
clase, con otros matices. (III,I; pp. 331-2)

La Sociedad de los Tres funcionó por las afueras y las Ventas, la Prosperidad y el barrio de Doña Carlota, el puente de Vallecas y los Cuatro Caminos, y si la existencia de esa sociedad no llegó a sospecharse ni a pasar a los anales del crimen, fue porque sus fechorías se redujeron a modestos robos, de los llamados por los profesionales *al descuido*. (III,IV; p. 347)

Of the places mentioned, those to the south (Casa de Campo, Carabanchel Bajo — but not Carabanchel Alto —, the Arroyo Abroñigal, the Puente de Vallecas and the Barrio de Doña Carlota) are in general at a lower level than Doña Casiana's boarding-house in the Calle de Mesonero Romanos — as is the Palacio Real —; those to the north and east (Tetuán, Cuatro Caminos, Prosperidad, La Guindalera, the Barrio de la Concepción and El Este) are in general at a higher level. La Elipa and Las Ventas, like the Calle de Mesonero Romanos, are at about 660 metres. This does not give notable support to Blanco Aguinaga's interpretation; rather the contrary. Add to this that Baroja nowhere places emphasis on the movement of characters upwards or downwards and one seems impelled to reject Blanco Aguinaga's view entirely. Nor is he helped by the evidence of the other two volumes in the trilogy, despite the general topographical movement upwards to the north. Thus, Baroja's description of the situation of the bar that gives its title to the third novel in the trilogy does not suggest that its altitude (680-90 metres) is associated with a notably better environment:

Hay entre Vallehermoso y el paseo de Areneros una ancha y extensa hondonada, que lentamente se va rellenando con escombros.

Estos terrenos nuevos, fabricados por el detritus de la población, son siempre estériles. Algunos hierbajos van naciendo en los que ya llevan aireándose algunos años. En los modernos, manchados de cal, llenos de cascote, ni el más humilde cardo se decide a poblarlos.

Por encima de estas escombreras pasan continuamente volquetes con tres y cuatro mulas, rebaños de cabras escuálidas, burros blanquecinos, chiquillos harapientos,

parejas de golfos que se retiran a filosofar lejos del bullicio
del pueblo, mendigos que toman el sol y perros vagabundos.
(*AR*, II,ɪ; p. 549)

The conclusion from so much evidence seems inevitable and
indisputable: Baroja in no way saw the topography of *La busca*
— or of *La lucha por la vida* — as symbolic; if he did, he was a
singularly inept writer.

We come now to alleged panoramas of repression. Seen from
below, says Blanco Aguinaga, Madrid appears as a 'ciudadela a
conquistar según se revela en el valor simbólico que parecen
adquirir, vistos desde abajo, la hoy catedral de la Almudena, el
Palacio Real y el Cuartel de la Montaña' (p. 237). He continues:

> Manuel—por ejemplo— veía con los ojos entornados los
> arcos de la iglesia de la Almudena por encima de una tapia;
> más arriba, el Palacio Real, blanco y brillante; los desmontes
> arenosos de la Montaña del Príncipe Pío, y su cuartel rojo y
> largo, y la hilera de casas del paseo de Rosales, con sus
> cristales incendiados por la luz del sol (p. 330). Ciudad, pues,
> que lleva en todo lo alto los símbolos de la Iglesia, Nobleza y
> Ejército (que también, según hemos visto, habían llamado la
> atención de Blasco); ciudad enemigo, para quienes la ven
> desde abajo; y ciudad, desde luego, bien defendida.
>
> A diferencia de los de abajo, los que están arriba pueden
> dejar vagar la vista por encima de 'la enorme desolación de
> los alrededores madrileños' (p. 457) hacia una agradable
> llanura de 'suaves ondulaciones' donde el Manzanares es
> 'como un hilo de plata' que se acerca al 'cerrillo de los
> Angeles' para luego perderse 'en el horizonte gris'. La vista es
> todavía más hermosa hacia el Noroeste [...]. (p. 237)

It is an attractive suggestion, especially since we know that
Baroja was notably critical of these three institutions. However,
despite Blanco Aguinaga's use of the words 'por ejemplo' to
introduce his quotation, and despite the presence in *La busca* of
many dozens of panoramic descriptions, this is the only one in
the book that brings together the trio of Church, Palace and
Barracks. Thus, the next extensive panoramic description to
appear after the one quoted by Blanco Aguinaga is the

following, two pages later, from near the Carretera de Andalucía, south of the Puente de Toledo (581 metres) and topographically one of the lowest points in the novel:

> Escanció Vidal en las copas y bebieron los tres.
>
> Se veía Madrid en alto, con su caserío alargado y plano, sobre la arboleda del Canal. A la luz roja del sol poniente brillaban las ventanas con resplandor de brasa; destacábanse muy cerca debajo de San Francisco el Grande los rojos depósitos de la Fábrica del Gas, con sus altos soportes, entre escombreras negruzcas; del centro de la ciudad brotaban torrecillas de poca altura y chimeneas que vomitaban, en borbotones negros, columnas de humo inmovilizadas en el aire tranquilo. A un lado se erguía el Observatorio, sobre un cerrillo, centelleando el sol en sus ventanas; al otro, el Guadarrama azul, con sus crestas blancas, se recortaba en el cielo limpio y transparente, surcado por nubes rojas. (III,I; 332-3)

Apart from denying Blanco Aguinaga support for the first of his two paragraphs quoted above, this description, in its last lines, clearly contradicts the view expressed in his second paragraph: namely that the pleasanter views over the surrounding countryside are confined to those above, 'a diferencia de los de abajo'. Indeed, Blanco Aguinaga's latter observation suggests a notable failure to understand the way in which Baroja repeatedly invokes nature: not as an indulgence for 'los que están arriba', but as a serene, though at times ominously holocaust-threatening ('nubes rojas') contrast to the sordid world of man (cf. above, pp. 36-7).

This brings us to the central problem of the study we are considering. Carlos Blanco Aguinaga is determined to see — and to make his reader see — everything in terms of class conflict and the oppression of the proletariat. As Baroja himself aptly remarked, 'Los socialistas, al menos los españoles, han creído siempre que todos son explotadores' (VII, 451). But Baroja does not see it in this way and cannot reasonably be made to do so. Except for a single house-breaking fiasco, the petty thieving and cheating and cruel pranks of the *golfos* — like the earlier bullying of Manuel by the guests in Doña Casiana's boarding-house ('Con el estudiante no se atrevían [...]; a Manuel le chillaba todo el mundo', p. 276) — are directed not against the strong but against the weak, against those who are scarcely in a better position than they themselves and are sometimes in a worse position: a family living in a hovel at the far end of the Dehesa de la Arganzuela from whom they steal a piece of cod; the young boy whose goat they steal; a youth whose pig they steal; a *paleto* whom they join with El Pastiri to cheat; El Cojo whose wooden leg they fling down the hillside; an old man whom they leave to freeze to death by lifting up the matting that protects him.... And in this, precisely, lies the cruelty of their actions and the anger and sense of pathos produced in the reader. Besides, 'la busca' of the title means many things. It points, most obviously, to the low-life world of 'los de la busca, randas y prostitutas' (p. 316), the *golfos*' search for whatever they can pick up and the prostitutes' search for clients. But other forms of search are relevant, too: Roberto's search for an inheritance and for people who may make it possible ('busco aquí...', p. 292; 'la que yo busco...', p. 306); Custodio's search for refuse ('A la busca', p. 356); the search for a meaning and direction in life: by Manuel ('no sabía qué hacer, ni qué camino seguir', p. 339), by Roberto ('Hay que buscar una ocasión y un fin para emanciparse de esta existencia mezquina', p. 341) and, potentially at least, by a host of others who live 'en las sombras de un sueño profundo, sin formarse idea clara de su vida, sin aspiraciones, ni planes, ni proyectos, ni nada' (p. 288). But where is the emphasis on search for work and economic security that Blanco Aguinaga's interpretation might lead us to expect? Blanco Aguinaga himself is strangely silent on the subject; Puértolas and Moral, both closely associated with Blanco Aguinaga's interpretation, offer little evidence and devote their main energies to supplementing Baroja on this point (above, p. 64); finally, Puértolas is manifestly mistaken when she writes, in line with a host of other commentators:

Varias veces a lo largo de *La busca* y *Mala hierba* Manuel intenta incorporarse al mundo del trabajo y de la honradez, y salir del ambiente de miseria material y espiritual que le rodea. Intenta alejarse de las malas compañías que lo arrastran al robo y al engaño, y buscar un empleo fijo, animado por las palabras de Roberto. (*20*, p. 89)

Apart from a momentary return to the bakery after his mother's death (p. 339), the only occasion in *La busca* where there is a suggestion that Manuel may have looked for work is in the sentence, 'Algunos céntimos que ganó subiendo maletas de las estaciones le permitieron ir viviendo, aunque malamente, hasta octubre' (p. 354), and this sort of work, as Baroja himself elsewhere pointed out, was part of the *golfo*'s 'busca' (V, 57). For the rest, work — in so far as Manuel does work — is simply thrust upon the boy by others and he is usually impatient with the resulting *sujeción*. In *Mala hierba* the position is even clearer: 'Manuel siguió sin buscar ni hacer nada útil' (p. 385). And when he is finally found (not finds) a respectable job as an apprentice compositor and has learnt his trade, he simply throws it up and goes off on the loose for several months with Jesús, during which time 'Ninguno de los dos se preocupaba en buscar trabajo' (p. 453). Only after Vidal's death, when he is being sought by the police, does he at last decide to look for a job himself and, despite Puértolas' and Moral's emphasis on the difficulty of such an enterprise in Madrid at the time, he is immediately successful: 'Manuel sintió en su alma bríos para comenzar una vida nueva: buscó trabajo y lo encontró en una imprenta de Chamberí' (p. 490). As simple as that. For the rest, the nearest one finds in *La busca* to a real quest for work is in the statement that Tío Patas came to Madrid 'a buscarse la vida' (p. 325), and it is made clear that by dint of hard work he succeeded. 'Ciudadela a conquistar'? It may well be so, but it is neither a capitalist fortress of social and economic privilege nor a topographical symbol of this. If there is a fortress to be conquered in *La busca*, it is primarily, I suggest, a psychological fortress — hence the repeated identification of the world of work with *sujeción* — and Manuel is prevented from conquering it by his idleness, by his much emphasized 'instinto antisocial de vagabundo' and by his notable lack of will power. This, at least, is how Baroja appears to have seen it. Certainly it is how he presents it in his novel.

Of course, it may well be that in this aspect of his work, as in his deflating of political ideologies in *Aurora roja*, Baroja is guilty of a 'profunda falsificación', in which case Blanco Aguinaga's repeated emphasis on the contrast between the 'planteamiento objetivo y realista de *La busca* y *Mala hierba*' (p. 271) and the 'escamateo ideológico' (p. 230) of *Aurora roja* is as mistaken as other aspects of his study, as indeed I believe it is. What is certain is that it is Baroja's actual trilogy that we are concerned with, not the hypothetical trilogy that a modern sociologist might wish he had written. Consequently, if there is evidence of departure from a basic standpoint of realism, it seems logical to look for an explanation in the internal structure and progression of the trilogy itself rather than to indulge in ideologically based vituperations of the novelist or admonitions on how the trilogy should have developed. As Blanco Aguinaga reminds us in his censure of Baroja, 'la realidad objetiva de la obra puede — y debe — imponerse a cualquier arbitrariedad del Dios que *no* es omnipotente' (p. 281). The observation may or may not be relevant to the novelist; it is certainly a valuable guide to the critic. Despite his repeated emphasis on documentation and realism Baroja did not accept that he was 'una máquina inerte e indiferente' (VII, 753). Nor would one wish him to have been so. The emphasis on *objetividad* and *objetivismo* has too often distracted attention from Baroja's greatness as a novelist. Baroja is not an objective writer. To emphasize objectivity as a basic characteristic of his writing and then to castigate the author for his lack of objectivity in those aspects of his writing that come into conflict with the critic's own assessment of Spanish history seems singularly perverse.

But Baroja is currently out of favour with a number of left-wing commentators and Blanco Aguinaga's study stands out as an attempt to find at least some merit in *La lucha por la vida* from a left-wing standpoint. A more regrettable reaction is nicely exemplified in an article by Francisco Carenas.[25] In that

[25] 'La abrumadora concreción del lenguaje barojiano', *Cuadernos Americanos*, 202 (September-October 1975), 116-27.

article the writer recounts how he himself evolved from 'incondicional admiración' for Baroja (for what seem to have been strikingly inadequate reasons: 'saciaba los personales deseos de este lector de desafío ante una sociedad pacata') to his 'frustrado repudio actual' (for equally inadequate reasons: 'Su concepto del hombre es demoledor, una especie de rémora preventiva de toda posibilidad de acción verdadera', though he thereupon seeks to justify his present standpoint by token literary analysis). The basic explanation for such changed taste, in Carenas as in others, seems to lie in the conjunction of Baroja's basic scepticism and the changed political situation in Spain. When the political system was oppressive, Baroja's 'invectivas' and 'falta de convicciones' were seen as banners of revolt against the prevailing 'farsa, hipocresía, intolerancia y fanatismo' (Carenas, p. 117) and the author was therefore heralded as a hero of the liberal cause, with the consequent inference of literary merit; with the coming of a more democratic system certain commentators have been dismayed to find that Baroja's scepticism about humans and their institutions is far wider and far deeper than they had realized, that it embraces democracy and socialism at least as much as other political systems, and that, now his works are no longer needed as a banner of revolt against an oppressive regime, Baroja is a singularly uncomfortable and discouraging companion to have with one in one's brave new world and therefore, it seems to be assumed, a bad writer. In short, certain left-wing politicizers today reject Baroja for reasons very similar to those traditionally found in right-wing commentators: for his scepticism about and his disparaging comments on basic aspects of their own ideological standpoints.[26]

[26] 'Baroja, de nuevo anatematizado' (in *Triunfo*, 507, 17 June 1972, p. 41) offers a good example of continuing right-wing distaste. The following is a brief sample quotation: 'Dios les haya perdonado (a Baroja, y también a Unamuno y a Ortega) el inmenso mal que han hecho y siguen haciendo en las mentes de nuestros jóvenes.'

In contrast to the eagerness of Left and Right to dissociate themselves from Baroja's scepticism and disillusion, one can recall the equally lamentable — and equally uncritical — eagerness of Left and Right to enlist into their ranks

After so many disagreements with Blanco Aguinaga and his followers it is pleasant to be able to respond warmly to their emphasis on the social injustices manifestly present in Madrid in the closing years of the nineteenth century and to their general enthusiasm for the acute observation and sensitive description that Baroja devoted to the consequences of such injustice. Nevertheless, Baroja's main emphasis is not on the injustice of society; it is on the bestiality of man. In this respect one can recall a review of *Mala hierba* written in 1904 by Azorín, Baroja's closest friend in the world of Spanish letters and probably the person who understood him better than anyone. At first sight, says Azorín, one may feel that Baroja's pessimism stems from social disorientation and iniquity, and the ingenuous reader may well attribute the novelist's bitterness to society's failure to overcome such injustice. Nothing could be further from the truth, continues Azorín. The root of Baroja's pessimism lies far deeper: not in social evils, which can be remedied, but in human nature itself, unchanging across the centuries. Baroja's pessimism is the pessimism of Hobbes, of Gracián, of Schopenhauer. Work, progress, education, human activity... they can change nothing essential. The more clearly one sees, the more profoundly one despairs, 'puesto que más claramente vemos y percibimos el desconcierto universal y su irremediabilidad perdurable' (Azorín, *OC* VIII, 2nd ed., 1963, 163-4). I find this view of Baroja very close to my own.

And yet one would perhaps venture to modify Azorín's interpretation in three respects. In the first place, as we shall see in Chapter 8, Baroja does not entirely exempt society from responsibility for the fate of its individuals, and we have already noted a considerable difference between his sympathetic presentation of El Expósito, condemned by society from the beginning, and his manifestly hostile presentation of El Bizco, all native animality and perversion (above, pp. 69-70). In the second place, as Blanco Aguinaga himself sees with manifest

the ingenuously optimistic, logic-chopping diagnosis of the problem of Spain propounded by Ganivet in *Idearium español*. See Ramsden, *Angel Ganivet's 'Idearium español'* (Manchester, 1967), pp. 21-30.

distaste, it is not just man who makes Baroja despair; it is very especially Spanish man and, beyond that, Latin man, Semitic man. In this respect the prologue that Baroja wrote for the Nelson edition of *La dama errante* is revealing: 'Aunque hoy se tiende, por la mayoría de los antropólogos, a no dar importancia apenas a la raza y darle mucha a la cultura, yo, por sentimiento más que por otra cosa, me inclino a pensar que el elemento étnico, aun el más lejano, es transcendental en la formación del carácter individual' (II, 229). Roberto Hasting, the most notable character of will and energy in *La busca*, is significantly part English. If only it were possible for Spaniards to show similar determination, Baroja seems to suggest, to 'llevar a cabo una obra diaria, de pequeñas molestias y de fastidios cotidianos' (pp. 341-2), then something might yet be done. But of course, for Baroja, with his characteristically *noventayochista* belief in unchanging national character, it is not possible. Hence the despair. In *Mala hierba* his view will become clearer. With his sculpture 'Los explotados', says Roberto, Alex 'quiere dar a entender que son los hombres a quienes agota el trabajo. Poco oportuno el asunto para España' (*MH*, p. 379). '¿Y qué piensas hacer?' he asks Manuel. 'Pues estar a lo que salga', replies the boy (*MH*, p. 379), an answer that contrasts nicely with Roberto's own attitude as expressed a few pages later: 'Yo no soy de los que están a lo que salga. No viene la montaña a mí, pues yo voy a la montaña; no hay más remedio' (*MH*, p. 382). '—Convierte tu vida estática en vida dinámica—' he tells Manuel; '—Quiero decir que tengas voluntad—'. Manuel contempló a Roberto desanimado. *Hablaban los dos en distinto idioma* (*MH*, p. 385; my italics). Manuel, free as ever from self-delusion, knows he is incapable of Roberto's will and energy: 'Es como si me dijesen que tuviera un palmo más de estatura' (*MH*, p. 385).

As the third and final proposed modification of Azorín's observations, I suggest that the word pessimism, a key word in all subsequent studies of Baroja's view of life, is too vague and calls for closer definition. Rather than depend on this large and imprecise blanket term, I prefer myself to refer to bitterness, disillusion, cheated optimism, inverted idealism. Basically, I suggest, Baroja is a puritan immersed in a world that falls sadly short of his desires. This point, too, I shall develop at length in Chapter 8.

7. Observation: (2) Further aspects of Madrid life

La busca stands out from other Spanish literature of the time by the author's acute observation and vivid portrayal of living conditions in the poor quarter of Madrid. As Baroja himself was later to observe, with apparent satisfaction, '*La busca* ha influido algo en la idea de las personas de posición acerca de los barrios pobres' (VII, 753-4). Nevertheless, exclusive emphasis on this aspect of the novel gives a rather limited view of the author's actual range and thereby tends to misrepresent the overall character of the work. In this chapter I shall consider a number of other documentary aspects that are commonly overlooked.

In the course of his writings Baroja referred repeatedly to his enthusiasm for traditional aspects of Spanish and especially Madrid life. Thus, in 1899, in a review of Maeztu's *Hacia otra España*, he decried the author's Europeanizing and regenerationalist approach, with emphasis on public health and straight streets, and observed: 'a nosotros nos enternece la debilidad, la pobreza y las callejuelas tortuosas, oscuras y en pendiente [...]; preferimos el pueblo que duerme al pueblo que vela' (VIII, 862). In the last lines of his review he pressed the point even more strongly:

> Es más: el día en que esa nueva España venga a implantarse en nuestro territorio, con sus máquinas odiosas, sus chimeneas, sus montones de carbón, sus canales de riego; el día en que nuestros pueblos tengan las calles tiradas a cordel, ese día emigro, no a Inglaterra, ni a Francia..., a Marruecos o a otro sitio donde no hayan llegado esos perfeccionamientos de la civilización. (VIII, 862)

In 1908, in *La dama errante*, Baroja made similar points through Iturrioz, in a long passage that is important for an understanding of the author's attitude in *La lucha por la vida*. Here I select only a few lines of special relevance to *La busca*.

Iturrioz is lamenting the changes that have taken place in
Madrid during the previous twenty-five or twenty-six years and
have left everything, now, 'apagado, gris':

> Madrid, entonces, era un pueblo raro, distinto a los demás,
> uno de los pocos pueblos románticos de Europa [...]. Todo el
> mundo se acostaba tarde; de noche, las calles, las tabernas y
> los colmados estaban llenos; se veían chulos y chulas con
> espíritu chulesco; había rateros, había conspiradores, había
> bandidos, había matuteros [...]. Entonces, los alrededores de
> la Puerta del Sol estaban llenos de tabernas, de garitos, de
> rincones, lo que permitía que nuestra plaza central fuera una
> especie de Corte de los Milagros [...]. Atraía lo pintoresco y lo
> inmoral [...]. Yo comprendo que aquella vida era absurda;
> pero, indudablemente, era más divertida. (II, 261)

Like his *alter ego* Luis Murguía, Baroja feels that 'la civilización
esteriliza el genio popular' (II, 926), and it is the 'genio popular'
that he himself wishes to discover. In 1926 he generalized his
own enthusiasms to the men of his generation as a whole:

> En las ciudades, los hombres de esta generación no
> buscarán las plazas elegantes, de aire parisiense o madrileño;
> preferirán visitar los barrios antiguos, los arrabales, y estarán
> siempre ansiosos de encontrar lo típico y lo característico. (V,
> 575)

Finally, in the second volume of his *Memorias*, 1944, he
observed:

> Otras ciudades españolas se habían dado cuenta de la
> necesidad de transformarse y de cambiar; Madrid seguía
> inmóvil, sin curiosidad y sin deseo de cambio. Por eso era un
> pueblo de gran interés [...]. Esta idea de la extrañeza de
> Madrid la he señalado varias veces, sin convencer,
> seguramente, a nadie. (VII, 574)

Thereupon, as evidence of his view, he quoted at length the
Iturrioz passage referred to above.

The emotive appeal of weakness, poverty and dark, twisting
streets 'en pendiente' — more relevant to *La busca*, I suggest,
than Blanco Aguinaga's proposed 'cuesta abajo' symbolism —,
the rejection of industrialization and modernization, the

concern for 'el genio popular', the attraction of 'lo pintoresco y lo inmoral', of the 'romantic' aspects of Madrid life, the delight in 'lo típico y lo característico', the finding of Madrid's appeal precisely in its 'estancamiento' and its 'fosilización' (VII, 574), in its 'extrañeza' ... in such a context, emphasis on Baroja as one well acquainted with 'la realidad social de un momento crucial de la fluctuación demográfica de la ciudad española en expansión capitalista' (*29*, p. 241) seems strangely irrelevant. Nor does Baroja seem to see the poverty aspects of Madrid as a new phenomenon brought about by immigration from the countryside. On the contrary, whatever the social and economic realities may have been, he himself apparently saw poverty as an emotion-prompting traditional aspect of Madrid life ('nos enternece la debilidad, la pobreza y las callejuelas tortuosas, oscuras y en pendiente'). Baroja, the most notable excursionist of his generation, according to another notable excursionist, Azorín (*OC*, VI, 229), was an excursionist in Madrid, too: a quester after 'lo típico y lo característico', a quester, very especially, after those aspects of Madrid life that cause 'extrañeza'. It is in this context, I suggest, that the evidence offered in Chapter 5 should properly be considered. Left-wing admirers of Baroja may be reluctant to accept the suggestion and, if they do accept it, may regrettably find that their admiration for him is diminished. Nevertheless, it is difficult to escape the fact: *La busca* is to a large extent a bringing together of the author's own excursionist observations, 'un conjunto de apuntes del natural' (VII, 753): people, living conditions, customs, entertainments.... In the pages that follow I propose to examine a number of aspects of this *excursionismo* that were not considered in Chapter 5.

I start with the most obviously tourist aspect: the world of entertainment. Part II, Chapter VII, offers the clearest evidence. One August night Leandro and Manuel go to a typical *kermesse* in the Calle de la Pasión. The word itself — even the type of *baile verbenero* to which it refers — is generally unknown to young people today, even in Madrid. During the last two decades the changing pattern of Madrid life — its regeneration as an industrial centre, greater wealth and sophistication, better transport out of the city, the Parque de Atracciones, the influx of immigrants from other parts of Spain, the gradual absorption of local *barrio* individuality into the growing impersonality and cosmopolitanism of the city as a whole — has almost completed the change that Iturrioz observed in 1908. Like so many of his descriptions Baroja's description of the *kermesse* stands out as a document from the past: the lanterns and flags and streamers and strings of light bulbs, the 'tómbola', the local band playing habaneras, pasodobles and schottisches, the 'ambigú' (another word that is generally unknown to young people today), the family groups, the *chulos* 'echándoselas de pollo[s]', the occasional 'arranque fanfarrón'.... When Leandro is finally exasperated by his girl friend's neglect, he goes off with Manuel to a 'café cantante' — another characteristic entertainment of the age — where there are two girls dancing: one dressed as a 'maja'; the other as a 'manolo'. 'Vamos de aquí—murmuró Leandro, después de breve rato—. Esto está muy triste [...]. En el café de la Marina habrá jolgorio.' So they leave and walk along the Calle de la Montera, past soliciting prostitutes 'con sus trajes claros' (another nice observation that has lost its significance now that other women are not invariably dressed in black), to the Café de la Marina, which Baroja describes at length: the place, its *cantaoras* who are also hostesses to the public, the inevitable *aficionado* holding forth on *cante*, and the performance itself, treated with a characteristically Barojan mingling of irony and caricature.

Later in the novel, while staying with Señor Custodio, Manuel is taken to a bullfight, another document from a bygone age, before the picador's horse had its present-day protective *peto*, with the consequence that Baroja describes: 'con todos los intestinos fuera, pis[ando] sus entrañas con los cascos'. As in the description of the *tablao flamenco* Baroja's treatment of the bullfight is notably deflating: the matador with his 'miedo terrible' ready to take to his heels, the 'pobre animal [...] con la lengua fuera, chorreando sangre, [que] miraba con ojos tristes de moribundo', and the applause of the public (which suggests that this is not an unusually bad bullfight). It is an extremely vivid description. It is also extremely emotive writing. Baroja, like other outstanding writers of the '98 Generation, shared Manuel's view of the *fiesta nacional* as 'una asquerosidad repugnante y cobarde': 'una fiesta en donde no se notaba más que el miedo del torero y la crueldad miserable del público recreándose en sentir la pulsación de aquel miedo' (p. 368).

The tourist in Madrid will hardly wish to miss a Sunday morning in the Rastro. Here, too, Baroja offers himself as a guide, in a passage that is regrettably too long to quote or to comment on (p. 345). It is, however, one of his most effective descriptions and, with its remarkable evocation of variety, confusion and hubbub, it is as vivid a document of Madrid life as the description of the Corralón or the description of the beggars at the Doctrina. Among the vividly presented individual representatives of this world one recalls especially El Pastiri, with his 'juegos de ballestilla' (p. 316), El Tabuenca with his 'rueda de barquillero' (p. 305), Don Alonso with his 'Torre Infiel' and his 'fonógrafo' (p. 306), Tío Pérquique announcing his cream cakes '¡A perra chica! ¡A perra chica!' (p. 348)....

Baroja, then, was clearly not interested only in the sordid living conditions of Madrid; he was interested also in its local colour and old-world picturesqueness. Behind both interests, I suggest, bringing the two together as aspects of the same phenomenon, lies the fascination for Baroja of 'lo típico y lo característico'. There is a host of supplementary evidence, much of it giving glimpses of Madrid that would be commonplace in Baroja's day and much of which was still familiar to the *madrileño* of twenty years ago: cows kept on the ground floor of blocks of flats, even near the centre of the city (p. 258); the 'sereno' locking doors at night (p. 316) and waking people in the morning (pp. 260, 325); the theatre claque (p. 352); men playing cards in the patio of a tenement building (p. 282) or outside taverns (p. 286); women combing their hair or their children's hair in the street (pp. 295, 345); mattress-remakers beating up the compacted wool in the Campillo de Gil Imón (p. 295); gas and oil and paraffin lighting (pp. 260-1, 295, 325, 327); a mule

turning the kneading-machine in the bakery (p. 327); rubbish
thrown into the street (p. 260); Madrid with its 'campos de
rastrojo' (p. 286).... Moreover, for the foreigner there are
delightful incidental pointers to aspects of Spanish life that the
average Spaniard still takes for granted, though in certain cases
less than he did a generation ago: the closeness of the family
unit, for example, as in Ignacio's household where the Sunday
meal brings together not only three generations but also a sister-
in-law (Salomé), whose children, incidentally, spend Sundays
with another relative, and Manuel, the son of a cousin, who has
already spent two years living with other relatives in Soria (pp.
282-3), a closeness not exempt, of course, from quarrels and
squabbles (p. 322); the importance of friends and personal
contacts, too (p. 303); the insistence on paying in bars even
though one can ill afford it (p. 299); people staring at strangers
— or simply at other people in general — and not hesitating to
ask questions about them (pp. 299-300); the importance of
cigarettes as a social contact phenomenon (p. 290) — like sundry
physical contact phenomena (kissing, embracing, touching,
back-slapping) —; significant gestures: 'haciendo un corte de
mangas' to indicate sexual proclivities (p. 285), '—[¿Mujeres
guapas?] ¡Uf..., así...!—contestó don Alonso, uniendo sus
dedos—' (p. 310), '—No, hombre; es que ya no puede
pasar—contestó [the drunken Pastiri], llevando la mano abierta
a la garganta' (p. 317) and, a moment later, 'dando en la manga
al Valencia con el revés de la mano' (p. 317).... In these cases as
in a host of others Baroja is a superb observer and a
correspondingly superb communicator of his observations.
Moreover, the 1903-4 revision offers abundant evidence of his
conscious striving in this direction. In the following lines, for
example, everything italicized was added in 1904:

> Manuel se sentaba sobre un baúl, y la vieja, *con el pitillo en
> la boca y echando humo por las narices*, contaba aventuras de
> sus tiempos de esplendor [...].
>
> —Porque, hijo, créelo—le decía—, una mujer que tenga
> *buenos* pechos y que sea *así* cachondona —*y la vieja daba una
> chupada al cigarro y explicaba con un gesto expresivo lo que*

entendía por aquella palabra no menos expresiva— siempre se llevará de calle a los hombres. (p. 269; my italics)

As in this specific example, so also in general, observation in 1904 appears more acute than in 1903, descriptions are more physical, and what is presented is correspondingly more immediate and more vivid.

Baroja's depiction of popular speech demands a paragraph to itself, especially in view of the 1903-4 revision. As a preliminary the following pair of examples will serve to illustrate the notably greater emphasis on direct speech in the later version of the novel:

1903 Pero Leandro le dijo que eso no estaba bien, porque los industriales todos tenían que ayudarse y que para eso se había inventado el socialismo, que era para favorecer la industria del hombre.

La vieja murmuró que ella se reía del socialismo. (*El Globo*, 11 March)

1904 —Pues no, señora—le replicó Leandro—. Eso no está bien.

—¿Por qué no?

—Porque no; porque los industriales tienen que ayudarse, y si usted hace eso, pongo por caso, impide usted que otra venda, y para eso se ha inventado el socialismo, para favorecer la industria del hombre.

—Bueno; pues que le den dos duros a la industria del hombre y que la maten. (p. 281)

For the rest one notes, especially in the 1904 version: the author's attempt to reproduce the pronunciation of popular Madrid speech (as in 'esos *cabayeros quien* hablar con *eya*', p. 317 ['Es que quieren hablar con ella' in 1903]; his frequent use of popular expressions (as in 'la *mare* que las ha *parío*', p. 293 ['la madre que las ha parido' in 1903]), of low-quarter *caló jergal* (as in 'najarse' [escaparse], 'jamar' [comer], 'afanar' [hurtar]),[27] of grammatical incorrections, especially *madrileñismos* (*laísmo*,

---

[27] Much increased in the 1903-4 revision. For example:

1903 —¡Toma, para venderlas! Se venden aquí en la puerta misma de la Doctrina á dos pesetas. (*El Globo*, 15 March)

1904 —¡Toma!, para pulirlas. Se venden aquí en la misma puerta a dos *chulés.* (p. 293)

'decían *veniría*, *saliría*, *quedría*'; the use of *aquí* for *éste*; the inverting of weak pronoun objects as in 'que no te se ocurra' [regrettably 'corrected' in the *OC* edition]...); the use of *zarzuela*-like *fanfarronadas* and *chulerías* (examples on pp. 311, 314-15, 318-19...), with much emphasis on such popular concerns as valour, fear, drink and money. In the following extract, which illustrates some of these points, everything after 'Que se casen ellas' was added in the 1903-4 revision:

> —¿Yo? ¡Que naranjas de la China! Que se casen ellas si *tien* con quien. Vienen aquí amolando con rezos y oraciones. Aquí no hacen falta oraciones, sino *jierro*, mucho *jierro*.
>
> —Claro, hombre..., *parné* [dinero], eso es lo que hace falta.
>
> —Y todo lo demás..., leñe y jarabe de pico...; pero *pa* dar consejos *toos semos* buenos; pero en tocante al *manró* [pan], ni las gracias.
>
> —Me parece. (pp. 293-4; the bracketed renderings are mine)

In all the above, as in the use of short sentences with relatively little subordination, Baroja's *La busca* marks a notable drawing close to real-life speech and, thence also, a significant step forward in Spanish literature.

I have so far omitted an important aspect of Madrid life: the bars of the poor quarter where still in the 1950s one could spend the night *de tascas* and finish up at 6 a.m. with *chocolate con churros* in the Plaza Mayor. La Blasa's tavern is a particularly vivid and debased example and it brings us close to the low-life conditions that were surveyed in Chapter 5. Indeed, it could well have been included there: with its prostitutes, its gypsies, its drunkards, its cardsharpers, its *chulos*, its homosexual, its knife fight, its supervising 'hipopótamo malhumorado'... and its vile brandy. But we are introduced to it in the company of Roberto and his cousin Fanny: Roberto with his repeated desire to make contact with low-life aspects of Madrid, and Fanny, 'una mujer original, una pintora, [que] tiene gana de ver algo de la vida pobre de estos barrios' (p. 299). 'Aquí miseria es lo único que se ve', says Leandro as he shows them the Corralón. '¡Oh, sí, sí!'

replies Fanny in evident delight, and her delight presumably continues in the subsequent visit to La Blasa's tavern. Certainly her interest does. It is the point in the novel where the squalid conditions illustrated in Chapter 5 and the more obviously picturesque, local-colour aspects surveyed in the present chapter come most closely together. Roberto's and Fanny's visit to the poor quarter is clearly *turismo de barrio bajo.* La Blasa's tavern, I suggest, is not there merely — or even principally — for its relevance to social conditions; it is there for its local colour and for the strong impact that it makes on the observer. Moreover, if we look back at the description of the *tablao flamenco* or the bullfight — or even the presentation of the three *chulos* and Leandro's response to them in the *kermesse* — we find something similar: the evocation by the author of characteristically strong responses, a means of communicating to the reader the 'extrañeza' that Baroja himself experienced in his contact with 'lo pintoresco y lo inmoral' of 'romantic' Madrid. But if this is true of La Blasa's tavern, may it not also be true of the Corralón, of the Corte de los Milagros, of the *golfos*' escapades, of the cave of La Montaña...? Emphasis on *La busca* as an objective portrayal of social conditions, with the accompanying neglect of other areas of similarly evocative writing, seems to the present writer to misrepresent the character of the novel, to distract attention from its emotive unity and, thence also, from Baroja's essentially non-objective and even obsession-ridden response to the world that he presents in *La busca.*

Among the areas of strong response characteristic of *La busca* are those of crime and immorality. Apart from being exemplified in the action of the novel, such areas are also much referred to in conversations: by Ignacio and his family (pp. 280-1, 283), by Vidal and El Bizco (p. 331), by the urchins huddled in the doorway of the Observatory (p. 337).... But the fascination with crime and immorality is not confined to the inhabitants of the poor quarter of Madrid. It is found also among the lodgers in Doña Casiana's boarding-house. Moreover, in their gossip about the 'célebre crimen de la calle de

Malasaña' (p. 272) they not only talk about crime; they also seek
to involve some of their fellow-lodgers in it. The corresponding
passage offers a good example of Baroja's use of real-life
documentation and merits consideration at length.

Doña Celsa Nebot was killed, we are told, and her body
soaked in paraffin and set fire to. The reference is clearly to one
of the most reported and discussed crimes of the late nineteenth
century in Spain: the crime of the Calle de Fuencarral,
immediately adjoining the Calle de Malasaña. On 1 July 1888
Doña Luciana Boncino, a wealthy widow, was murdered and, as
with the fictitious Doña Celsa Nebot, her body was soaked in
paraffin and set fire to. Her maid was the principal suspect but
the widow's son had a record of crime and violence and, though
he was officially in prison on the date of the murder, reports and
rumours suggested that he had been seen out of prison at the
time and these led to the suspension from duty of the prison
governor. Who had committed the murder and tried to burn the
body? What had become of the victim's jewels and the large sum
of money that she had recently withdrawn from the bank? Had
the son really been seen out of prison at the time of the murder?
If so, was he implicated in the crime and was the prison governor
himself an accomplice? During the long months of police
investigation the national and local press informed, sought out
witnesses and café tittle-tattlers, hypothesized, fantasized, pre-
judged questions of guilt, confused justice with politics, and
managed to keep public interest and emotions at fever pitch.
Galdós reported on developments at length in a series of
newspaper articles[28] and Baroja was fascinated by public
reactions to the crime: a 'caso de psicología popular [...]. ¡Qué
folletín! ¡Qué novela por entregas viva!' (VII, 568). In *La busca*

[28] Subsequently gathered together and published posthumously in book form:
El crimen de la calle de Fuencarral (Madrid, 1928; not in *OC*). Baroja seems
to have known these articles and it is interesting to compare his treatment
with Galdós's: the most notable similarity is in the evocation of the resulting
gossip and rumour-mongering, 'el campo inmenso de las más extrañas
conjeturas, (Galdós, *El crimen*, p. 44); the most notable difference is one of
tone (whereas Baroja deflates with humour, Galdós condemns from a
sterner, more characteristically Victorian moral standpoint).

he brings out nicely the sort of scandal-mongering that became rife:

> En el famoso proceso de la calle de Malasaña, una criada declaró que una tarde vio al hijo de doña Celsa en un aguaducho de la plaza de Oriente hablando con un viejo cojo. Para los huéspedes, el tal hombre no podía ser otro que don Telmo. Con esta sospecha, se dedicaron a espiar al viejo [...].
> —Indudablemente—dijo el Superhombre—, don Telmo mató a doña Celsa Nebot; la vizcaína fue la que regó el cadáver con petróleo y le pegó fuego, y Roberto, el que guardó las alhajas en la casa de la calle de Amaniel. (p. 273)

Galdós, in one of his reports, observed how the press was divided in its attitude: on the one hand there was responsible reporting of the investigatory process, without comments; on the other hand, there was irrational anger at the process, with a totally biased selection of evidence. 'De la discusión entre los órganos de estas dos tendencias han salido las denominaciones de *sensatos* e *insensatos*, con que los periódicos de uno y otro bando se designan' (*El crimen*, p. 41).[29] Baroja's presentation of a comparable division in the occupants of Doña Casiana's boarding-house is therefore more humorous than it might at first appear (p. 273). The humour consists in a characteristic example of Barojan deflation: terminology associated with debate at a national level is applied to the here-and-now world of a low-class boarding-house. It is obviously comparable to the juxtaposition, in II,I, of 'la regeneración nacional' and 'la regeneración del calzado', but with a significant difference: in the latter juxtaposition the contrasting planes ('nacional' and 'del calzado') are both present in the text and the humour of contrasted registers in the word 'regeneración' is therefore immediately apparent, even if one knows little or nothing of the *regeneracionista* context of the time; in the former juxtaposition, on the other hand, only the low-class boarding-house register of the duality *sensatos/insensatos* is present in the text; the national-press register — and consequently also much

[29] Compare Baroja's own later observation: 'Los periódicos españoles se dividieron en sensatos e insensatos' (VII, 568).

of the humour of the juxtaposition — depends on the reader's awareness of the context of press reports and dissensions. Similarly, Senabre has suggested that, within the 'Regeneración del calzado' passage, 'el "hermoso león amarillo con cara de hombre y melena encrespada" es, naturalmente, una transposición caricaturesca de Costa' (*37*, p. 396). If that is so, it is another example of the reader's need for awareness of specific contemporary references. In the 'Sociedad de los Tres' formed by Vidal, El Bizco and Manuel (p. 333) there is perhaps an even more extreme — and characteristically disillusioned — in-joke: with a reference to the ephemeral regenerating group 'los Tres' formed by Baroja, Azorín and Maeztu.

In examining Baroja's treatment of the 'célebre crimen de la calle de Malasaña' we have passed from an area of strong responses, as in the description of the bullfight or the description of La Blasa's tavern, to an area of humour, and the ground is almost prepared for the following chapter. The last example of documentation reminds us of yet another characteristic area of *La busca* that is commonly overlooked. I refer to the extravagant and eccentric and take as my illustration Roberto's quest for a denied inheritance. Despite the student's adscription to the 'sensatos' in Doña Casiana's boarding-house his claim that he will one day inherit 'muchísimo..., millones...' (p. 274) does not carry great conviction with other characters in the novel, including the reader's principal guide, Manuel, who most commonly responds with surprise and irony (pp. 292, 294, 305) and with inner reflections on Roberto's mental state (pp. 292, 339, 341). Moreover, the author encourages similar responses in the reader, both by the contrast he repeatedly establishes between Roberto's illusions and his present position and by the imagery through which Roberto expresses himself (both exemplified in 'los cimientos de mi obra y el andamiaje están hechos; ahora el caso es que necesito dinero', p. 274). In his presentation of Roberto, as in so many other aspects of the novel, Baroja's treatment is notably deflating. The following exchange takes place in the beggars' food queue at the María Cristina barracks:

—[...] Figúrate tú, cuando yo coja esa cantidad, lo que van

a ser para mí estos cochecitos y estas cosas. Nada.

—Y ahora, mientras tanto, no tiene usted una perra.

—Así es la vida; hay que esperar, no hay más remedio. Ahora que nadie me cree, gozo yo más con el reconocimiento de mi fuerza que gozaré después con el éxito. He construido una montaña entera; una niebla profunda impide verla; mañana se desgarrará la niebla y el monte aparecerá erguido, con las cumbres cubiertas de nieve.

Manuel encontraba necio estar hablando de tanta grandeza cuando ni uno ni otro tenían para comer, y, pretextando una ocupación, se despidió de Roberto. (p. 343)

Roberto, then, is clearly presented as as eccentric, 'chiflado, pero [de] buen corazón' (p. 339), and he fits nicely into the context of Madrid's 'vida absurda' that so appealed to Iturrioz and Baroja. But the tale of his mysterious inheritance also illustrates Baroja's use of documentation, for the tale is clearly rooted in real-life experience: in the story of an inheritance to which the Baroja family itself might conceivably have had some claim. Baroja's account of the circumstances, in his *Memorias* (VII, 521-2), is remarkably similar to Roberto's (pp. 274-5, I,IV; 342, III,III) and the reader is urged to compare them. There is, however, also, a notable contrast: whereas Roberto pursued his inheritance, Baroja did nothing: 'Naturalmente, yo no hice nada, porque no tenía datos concretos y hubiera perdido el tiempo y el dinero' (VII, 522). There is therefore nothing in the real-life story of the Baroja inheritance corresponding to Roberto's quest or to his subsequent discovery of a forgery in a parish register perpetrated by Shaphter, an agent of a rival claimant. Baroja has elaborated a fantasy of what might have been.

And yet, even in that elaboration he drew on real-life material: perhaps on the character of his friend Paul Schmitz with his enthusiasm for Nietzsche — in the energy of Roberto's quest —; almost certainly on the much reported Sackville affair for certain details of the quest: the large inheritance that was at stake; the aristocratic social position of those involved, which may have prompted Baroja's reference to Roberto as a 'tipo

aristocrático' (p. 274); the combination of long search in Spain
and protracted litigation in the English Courts; the forging of a
parish register; the unusual *ph* in the name of the real-life forger,
Rophon, which may have suggested the equally unusual *ph* in
the name of Baroja's forger, Shaphter; the fact that the real-life
claimant was from South Africa, which must surely have given
Baroja the idea of Roberto's father, 'un calavera que se escapó
de su casa' and died in Australia (pp. 342-3).[30] In short, in
elaborating a fantasy of his own possible quest for a lost
inheritance, it seems fairly sure that Baroja found suggestions
and details in a real-life contemporary quest. As Baroja himself
remarked: 'Para mí, la condición primera del escritor es la
exactitud. La medida exacta en lo que es medible, hasta en lo
que es fantasía' (VII, 812).

[30] For further details, see the almost daily reports on the Sackville affair in the
Spanish press (notably *El Imparcial*) from 31 October to 14 November 1901.
See also the subsequent account by Victoria Sackville-West in her book
Pepita (London, 1937). Significantly, a contemporary reviewer of *La busca*
recalled immediately 'el asunto Sakville' [sic] as the source of Roberto's quest
(*14*, pp. 121-2).

8. Emotion: selection and orchestration

Despite his repeated and clearly justified emphasis on the documentary aspect of his novels, Baroja — with specific reference to *La busca* — rejected the suggestion that he was 'una máquina inerte e indiferente que pudiera registrar lo que pasara delante de ella' (VII, 753). Complete objectivity, he believed, was impossible: 'Yo no he visto dos personas que hayan sido testigos de un mismo hecho [y] lo recuerden de la misma manera; cada uno le da su carácter, y, con su carácter, su pasión y su manera de ser peculiar' (VII, 494). Besides, he declared elsewhere — in the same passage that was quoted earlier to illustrate his claim to documentary value —, his own 'fondo dionisiaco' and 'tendencia turbulenta' prevented him from being a 'contemplador tranquilo': 'y, al no serlo, tengo, inconsciente-mente, que deformar las cosas que veo, por el deseo de apoderarme de ellas, por el instinto de posesión, contrario al de contemplación' (II, 229). It is this essentially subjective aspect of *La busca* that I am concerned with in the present chapter.

The world of work offers a useful starting-point. As we have seen, Baroja places little emphasis on it and Puértolas and Moral, in the corresponding sections of their background surveys, devote their main energies to supplementing Baroja's evidence. Moreover, where the world of work does appear in *La busca* it is invariably in a subordinate role: either for the light it throws on Manuel's character or situation, or as a mere starting-point for the presentation of certain areas of experience that seem to have had a special fascination for Baroja. Most commonly it serves both these ends at the same time.

I start with subordination to Manuel's character or situation. His experience of work in Doña Casiana's boarding-house is an obvious example; so is his experience of work in Tío Patas' shop. In both cases there is less emphasis on work than on the boy's response to work, with the usual interplay between

sujeción and *vagabundaje*. Moreover, in Tío Patas' shop Baroja
clearly sacrifices the work aspect to the *sujeción* aspect. Thus,
having described all the work that Manuel had to do in the
morning, he continues: 'Por la tarde era más pesado el trabajo:
Manuel tenía que estarse quieto detrás del mostrador,
aburriéndose, vigilado por el ama y su cuñada. Acostumbrado a
los paseos diarios por las rondas, le desesperaba tal inmovilidad'
(p. 325). Similarly, we glimpse the world of work for a moment
as Manuel and Vidal return home from the *zapatería*: 'a lo largo
de las rondas marchaban en cuadrillas los obreros de los talleres
próximos' (p. 295). But thereafter our attention is immediately
diverted to Manuel's and Vidal's constant talk of women and
money, and the workers, in retrospect, appear as a contrasting
background. Similarly again, in III,I, after Manuel has been
assured by Vidal that work is '*pa* el gato' and Baroja has
commented on El Bizco's scorn for 'la ley del trabajo', 'pasaron
por la carretera un hombre y una mujer con un niño en brazos'.
They are going to the mills, says Vidal. It is a superbly pathetic
scene. But it serves again, principally, to throw light on Manuel
and his companions who, immediately afterwards, 'estuvieron
más de una hora hablando de mujeres y de medios de sacar
dinero' (p. 332). Finally, even in the three main areas of work
actually described in *La busca* one finds something similar: in
the *zapatería*, where 'la monotonía en el trabajo y la sujeción
atormentaban a Manuel' though he gradually got used to it (p.
282); in the bakery, where, apart from *sujeción*, the boy
experienced also lack of affection, another recurring element in
the novel (pp. 326-7); at Custodio's, where the importance of
these same two elements, *sujeción* and affection, is emphasized
yet again (pp. 359, 372). Of these three examples, that of the
bakery is especially revealing. It offers the most vivid description
of work in the whole novel and is the only one referred to by
both Puértolas and Moral. Nevertheless, it is still subordinated
to the presentation of Manuel's individual situation — to such
an extent that part of that situation, the ill-treatment of him by
his fellow workers, 'una colección de gallegos bastante brutos',
prevents the reader from extending his own sympathy to those

fellow workers (as Moral would have us do) and thereby banishes the potential class significance and impact of the work described. The bakery episode, then, where work is most vividly evoked, is a particularly good example of the essentially subordinate role of work in *La busca.*

Work in *La busca* is subordinated not only to the presentation of characters; it is subordinated also, more peculiarly, to certain areas of experience that seem to have held a special fascination for Baroja. As in his presentation of characters so also in his presentation of these characteristically Barojan areas, often in the same examples, the author evokes the world of work, usually very briefly, but thereupon diverts the reader's attention away from it. There are three notable directions of diverted attention: human bestiality, picturesque eccentricity or extravagance, and local-colour aspects of Madrid life.

As an example of the first I recall the description of Salomé and the reference to her world of work. The corresponding passage was considered at length in Chapter 3 and we observed how Salomé's niceness serves Baroja, by contrast, to bring out the brutality of her husband. Within that niceness, arousing our sympathy, is her hard work for little reward, 'cosiendo a máquina, a cinco céntimos las dos varas'. One can, if one wishes, here recall the derisory rates paid for female labour at that time (*21*, pp. 158-61). But that is not where Baroja's emphasis lies. Work is here clearly subordinated to something that concerns Baroja far more, human bestiality, and attention has been drawn to the increased emphasis of such bestiality in the definitive version of the novel. Several of the examples referred to earlier in this chapter offer similar evidence: the workers returning from the 'talleres próximos', used as an effective background to Manuel's and Vidal's constant talk of women and money (p. 295); the man, woman and child going to the mills, used to bring out the callousness of El Bizco and Vidal — Manuel being saved somewhat by the indication that he watched the family 'con pena' (a 1904 addition) — (p. 332); Manuel's work in the bakery, made more onerous by the ill-treatment of his brutish fellow workers (p. 327).

As an example of the diverting of attention from work to eccentricity and extravagance I take II,IV. There are two examples in immediate succession. In the first there is a brief reference to Rebolledo *padre* and his work as a barber, though even here the emphasis is on his 'anuncio humorístico' rather than his work; thereafter our attention is immediately diverted to his even more picturesque spare-time activities (pp. 296-8). Then the Aristas brothers are presented. They are apprentices in a metal foundry, we are told. What potential if Baroja really had been concerned with the working conditions of the proletariat at a time of capitalist expansion! But this is not his concern and we are told nothing of work in the foundry. We are told, however, about the Aristas brothers' out-of-work enthusiasms: the younger brother's for gymnastics; the older brother's for anything concerned with death (p. 298). Two passages referred to earlier in a different respect offer similar evidence: over half the Tío Patas episode is devoted to the shopkeeper's 'historia [...] verdaderamente interesante'; over half the bakery episode is devoted to the portrait of another typically Barojan 'character', Karl the German baker.

Finally, as an example of the diverting of attention from work to local-colour aspects of Madrid life, I take Manuel's stay with Custodio and his wife. In fact, his stay there exemplifies also all the aspects of diverted attention so far considered: the situation and response of Manuel (see above, p. 106); human brutality (most notably in the bullfight, pp. 367-8); picturesque eccentricity (to a certain extent, Custodio himself, pp. 361-2; more obviously, El Conejo, pp. 362-4). But it serves Baroja also as a starting-point for the presentation of local-colour aspects of Madrid life: El Carnicerín, a classic *chulo* type (pp. 366-7), the bullfight (pp. 367-8) and a local *barrio* wedding (p. 369).

Baroja, then, having pointed to the world of work, usually very briefly, thereupon directs attention away from it: either to the situation or response of characters in the novel — most commonly a response of impatience with its *sujeción* or even outright rejection of it — or to one of three areas that seem to hold a special fascination for him. In the former case it is characters who react against work in favour of more pleasurable pastimes; in the latter case it is the author himself. Is the similarity significant? May we say that characters reject work because the author rejects it, because he himself is impatient with this aspect of changing Madrid, 'apagado, gris' (VII, 575)? It is a tempting hypothesis. Of course, one can think of other possible factors, too: most notably, that Baroja, who described 'por impresión directa' (VII, 1053), did not himself know the working world of the proletariat and therefore could not describe it. But nor did he, by his own social position, know the world of the *golfos*. In the former case he made no attempt to overcome his ignorance; in the latter case he did. Moreover, as we have seen, even when he presents an aspect of work that he does know, that of the bakery, he still subordinates it to other things. One finds exactly the same thing in *Mala hierba* and *Aurora roja* with another area of work that was well known to him, that of newspaper offices and printing-shops, and no sooner does Manuel become established as the owner of his own printing-shop in *Aurora roja* than he appoints a manager and thereafter spends his time in the colourful company of anarchists and others of similar offbeat appeal. There seems little doubt about it, then: the modern world of work holds little attraction for Baroja; on the other hand, human bestiality, human eccentricity and local-colour aspects of Madrid life fascinate him. In the preceding pages I have used the world of work, much emphasized by certain commentators, as a yardstick of that fascination and I have pointed out that it never appears except when subordinated to other things. Those other things, however, do appear — frequently — without reference to the world of work. The latter, then, has served its purpose and can henceforth be left aside. We can also leave aside the question of Manuel's character and situation which was sufficiently considered in Chapter 4. Far more interesting for my present purpose are those three areas of peculiarly Barojan emphasis: bestiality, eccentricity and local colour.

Bestiality — or simple lack of basic humanity — is much emphasized in *La busca*: the bullying and spite-venting by the guests in Doña Casiana's boarding-house (p. 276), Leandra's immoral views on life (p. 283), the Piratas and their marauding (pp. 284-5), El Bizco's and Vidal's callous disregard for others (p. 332), the 'mala intención' that shocks Manuel during the night he spends with the *golfos* (p. 337), the feeling of deprived affection that runs through Manuel's various experiences.... Roberto's comment at the Doctrina is relevant:

> —[...] ¿Te has fijado?—añadió— ¡Qué pocas caras humanas hay entre los hombres! En estos miserables no se lee más que la suspicacia, la ruindad, la mala intención, como en los ricos no se advierte más que la solemnidad, la gravedad, la pedantería. Es curioso, ¿verdad? Todos los gatos tienen cara de gatos, todos los bueyes tienen cara de bueyes; en cambio, la mayoría de los hombres no tienen cara de hombres. (pp. 291-2)

In *El mayorazgo de Labraz* another Englishman, 'lo más que puede ser un hombre' (I, 69), makes very similar observations on the inhabitants of Labraz: thus, of the men, 'unos me recuerdan un caballo; otros, un mono o un perro; hay algunos que tienen movimientos de buey, como el notario; otros parecen búhos o papagayos'; and of the women, 'hay unas que parecen perrillos falderos; otras muchas tienen cara de gato; pero lo que más me desagrada es ver lo que abunda en ellas: el recuerdo de la cara de un cerdo' (I, 79). This, I suggest, is not merely a character talking; it is the author himself. And lest there should be any doubt about this, the abundance of animal imagery used to characterize people (over fifty examples in *La busca*, many of them added in 1904) is there to press the point: Doña Violante, 'aplastada como un sapo' (p. 267), 'aquel montón de mendigos [...] bullía como una gusanera' (p. 291), La Blasa, 'aquel hipopótamo malhumorado' (p. 300)...

Animal imagery in *La busca* does not serve only to indicate bestiality; it may also, very occasionally, point to more pleasant qualities: Milagros, 'fina como un pajarito' (p. 289), Perico Rebolledo '[que] parecía, como suele decirse, un ratón debajo de una escudilla' (p. 297). It is a shorthand characterization technique and an aspect of Baroja's attempt to prompt immediate emotive responses in the reader — as, indeed, he does in other ways, too: 'En una mesa de al lado, un hombre con trazas de chalán discutía acerca del cante y del baile flamenco con un bizco de cara de asesino' (p. 313; a 1904 addition). Underlying this feature of his writing, no doubt, is the author's own immediate emotive response to people and his repeatedly stated conviction that he had never been mistaken in that initial response. Similarly, in *Aventuras, inventos y mixtificaciones de Silvestre Paradox* Ossorio tells Paradox: 'yo clasifico a las personas en dos clases: una la forma la gente de mirada limpia y de cara abierta; la otra, los que tienen la mirada turbia y la cara cerrada' (II, 127). It is clearly the latter who predominate in Baroja's writings; the author's most frequent response to people, in his novels as in real life, is one of disgust:

> El anarquista teórico cree que el hombre es bueno y que todas las imposiciones de los códigos son perjudiciales. Esta es la herencia de Juan Jacobo Rousseau. Yo no creo en nada de esto; por el contrario, por instinto y por experiencia, creo que el hombre es un animal dañino, envidioso, cruel, pérfido, lleno de malas pasiones, sobre todo de egoísmos y de vanidades. (VII, 414)

'Extraordinario realismo objetivo'? Whoever thinks so must surely have a view of mankind as depressing as Baroja's own. In the words of the woodcutter in *El mayorazgo de Labraz*: 'Muchas veces oí decir que otro mundo hay en donde todo el mundo vive queriéndose y sin hacerse daño. No lo creo, ni lo creeré nunca [...]. Los osos y los lobos, las zorras y los pájaros, los hombres y las comadrejas, todos matan y hacen daño; es su regla' (I, 155).

Nevertheless, Baroja clearly suffers from the absence of that 'otro mundo' referred to by the woodcutter. Hence his anger and his bitterness. It is the cheated optimism of one who, despite the admitted sadness of his writing, declared, 'en el fondo de mi alma amo ardientemente la vida' (V, 48); a form of inverted idealism, like that of Karl the German baker who, in moments of depression, toppled from his world of ideals, saw everything as 'negro y desagradable' (p. 328). It is also the puritanical streak that Baroja noted in his mother (VII, 525) and that he pointed to repeatedly in himself ('una fuerte aspiración ética', II, 230; 'por exageración de puritanismo', V, 871; 'una fiebre de justicia aguda' VII, 436). And because of his high puritanical demands and expectations, Baroja finds the world around him corrupt, evil, diseased. His novel is filled with Goyaesque etchings of physical and moral degradation. Life is cruel; men are cruel. It is a jungle world of preying animals. When they are not actually at each other's throats their relationship is most commonly one of indifference or mockery or scorn or hatred. Charity is almost totally absent. Characters are 'petulantes', 'malhumorados', 'brutales', 'desafiadores', 'iracundos', 'desagradables', 'repugnantes', 'bestiales', and they shock with their 'mala intención' or with their 'brutalidad y animalidad repelentes'. In the final lines of the Corralón chapter Baroja sums up human relationships there:

Odios de personas de vida casi común, no era raro que fuesen de un encono y de un rencor violento; así, los de una y otra familia no se miraban sin maldecirse y sin desearse mutuamente las mayores desgracias. (p. 290; a 1904 addition)

Of course, as Baroja himself makes clear, social conditions have played a part. And yet, despite everything, not such a very great part. Thus, despite the 'comunismo del hambre' of the Corralón and the 'continuo aplanamiento producido por la eterna e irremediable miseria' (pp. 287-8), despite the description of the women in the Corralón as 'agriadas por la vida áspera y sin consuelo ni ilusión' (p. 289), despite Roberto's reflection in La Blasa's tavern, 'Sería curioso averiguar [...] hasta qué punto la miseria ha servido de centro de gravedad para la degradación de estos hombres' (p. 301), despite the sympathetic presentation of El Expósito, condemned by society from the beginning (pp. 335-6)... — despite these and other pointers to the part that social conditions have played in human degradation, Baroja's ultimate emphasis is on man's innate brutality and the impossibility of any real change, either in that or in the associated living conditions ('la eterna *e irremediable* miseria', with the words italicized by me added in the 1904 version to make his view quite clear). Hence the animal imagery by which characters are so often identified; hence the use of work, not for its own sake, but to bring out this brutality; hence, too, the following superbly pathetic passage from the description of the death of Petra:

> Ya había confesado a la Petra el cura de la casa una porción de veces. Las hermanas de Manuel iban de vez en cuando por allí, pero ninguna de las dos traía el dinero necesario para comprar las medicinas y los alimentos que recomendaba el médico. (p. 333)

This is Baroja at his best: no explicit commentary; biblical austerity of emotion and expression. And yet, what a world of injustice, too! For the reader of today, of course, it is a cruel reminder of the lack of free medical attention. This, however, is surely not Baroja's main point. Manuel's sisters were both working, yet neither of them brought the money necessary to buy medicine and food. It is another example, then, of the author's puritanical disgust with selfish, unfeeling humanity, and the prime target of his disgust is not the social system; it is individuals. One thinks again of Roberto's observation: 'Todos los gatos tienen cara de gatos, todos los bueyes tienen cara de bueyes; en cambio, la mayoría de los hombres no tienen cara de hombres.' What Roberto says of faces can be applied equally, in Baroja's world, to the heart within. For Baroja there are few humans with human hearts. It is perhaps his most recurrent obsession. Manuel's concern with affection and the difficulty that he has in finding it are clearly reflections of the author's own view of life.

As though in flight from this world of human insensitivity Baroja presents a number of picturesque, eccentric and even fantastic characters, scenes and episodes. In the previous chapter I considered Roberto and his 'misterios' (p. 310) and at the beginning of this chapter I referred briefly to several examples of eccentricity to which the author directs the reader's attention from the world of work: most notably, 'los Rebolledos, padre e hijo', the Aristas brothers and El Conejo. It is probable that in these cases as in the story of Roberto's inheritance Baroja drew on real-life experiences and observations: Rebolledo *padre*'s conversion of a serviette ring into a pair of false teeth, for example; Rebolledo *hijo*'s drawing of Don Tancredo; the younger Aristas' gymnastic enthusiasm and capers; the elder Aristas' 'necromanía aguda'.... Certainly one can still today hear a version of El Conejo's adaptation of the mass (p. 363). But more important than the possible documentary value of these characters and episodes is the fact that they all represent a notably characteristic feature of Baroja's writing, both in *La busca* and elsewhere: delight in the picturesque, the eccentric, the absurd, the extravagant, the fantastic. At times the corresponding characters are physically deformed: Rebolledo *padre*, for example, was 'contrahecho de cuerpo, enano y jorobado' (p. 296); El Tabuenca 'tenía una nariz absurda, una nariz arrancada de cuajo y sustituida por una bolita de carne' (p. 304); El Conejo, apart from his 'tic especial, un movimiento convulsivo de la nariz [que] agitaba su rostro de vez en cuando' and which gave him his name, was also a 'jorobado' (pp. 362-3). At other times they are simply picturesque or strange or comical: Señor Zurro, for example, a 'tipo pintoresco y curioso' (p. 289); Fanny, 'una mujer original [...] con tan extrañas trazas' (pp. 299-300); Don Alonso, with his 'aspecto cómico, mezcla de humildad, de fanfarronería y de jactancia triste' (p. 306).... For the most part, such characters appear for a moment at the focus of attention, vividly portrayed, and then disappear and take no further part in the novel; at times they are not even present in the flesh, but are depicted only in a story or an anecdote, as in the 'historias y anécdotas' of Don Alonso (p. 320). The most common reaction to them — of Manuel, of other characters and of the reader — is one of 'extrañeza' or 'asombro'. And it is not only in *La busca* and other novels (for example: I, 203-5, 215-18; II, 87-90, 92-3) that one finds such emphasis on anecdotes and extravagance; it is also in the author's *Memorias* where one finds frequently such words as 'pintoresco', 'ocurrente', 'fantástico', 'raro', 'curioso', 'original', 'misterioso', 'extraño', 'extraordinario' to introduce a given character or incident. Of course, Baroja emphasized repeatedly the need for 'amenidad' in one's writings and, in *La busca* at least, picturesque characters and episodes are nicely interspersed with more soul-searing descriptions so that the lighter episodes allow a relaxation of tension and, at the same time, stand out against the darker episodes in mutual contrast. But beyond any mere sop to the reader and beyond constructional relevance one feels that such episodes also had a powerful psychological appeal for Baroja. 'Para mí', he observed, 'una de las cosas más tristes de España es que los españoles no podamos ser frívolos ni joviales' (V, 49). His indulgence in extravagance, I suggest, is a desperate attempt of his own to cast aside his dark vision of life and to be, for a moment, 'frívolo' and 'jovial'.

But if Baroja experienced such repugnance for human bestiality, why did he need to take refuge in extravagance — or anything else? Why not simply turn his back on it as he did on the world of work? Why bring it so insistently to the forefront of his stage? The author himself points to an answer in a reference to one of his most perverted characters, 'el hermano Juan [a real-life character depicted in *El árbol de la ciencia*], con su vida enigmática y misteriosa, con sus instintos anormales contenidos'. What an 'historia admirable' for a novelist, he exclaims: 'este hermano Juan quizá era una basura humana, pero tan auténtica como basura y como humana, que produce tanta curiosidad como horror' (VII, 596). Being the puritan he is, Baroja is both repelled and fascinated by this specimen of authentic humanity, just as Manuel is both entertained and terrified by El Aristón and his necromania (p. 319). Like Karl the baker, it seems, Baroja needs 'excitantes [...] fuertes' (p. 328). As Landínez observed with reference to Ossorio in the largely autobiographical *Camino de perfección*, 'lo que a él le importa, sin duda, es [...] toparse con algo nuevo, excitante, que le sacuda, aunque sea sólo por un rato, el aburrimiento' (*10*, I, p. 120). Human brutality, like its opposite and complementary pole, human eccentricity, helps to satisfy that need. I find strong support for this suggestion in a purely incidental point that Baroja made in his 1899 review of Maeztu's *Hacia otra España*.

I can understand, he says, that a writer should give himself up to the probing of dark passions, but I cannot understand that he should press upon us annoying ideas of regeneration. It is the first part of this statement that concerns us here:

> Comprendo muy bien que un pensador se entretenga en desgarrar las conciencias, en disecar las pasiones, en mostrar las rencillas del odio, del egoísmo, de la miserable vanidad que se ramifican por nuestro espíritu. En ese dolor sentido hay una satisfacción cruel, una voluptuosidad intensa. (VIII, 861-2)

I find the last sentence especially significant. It is one of those revealing confessions that gives a critic a thrill. One has read *La busca*; one feels one has responded to it as a total work of art; one has read, without conviction, critics who present different interpretations of the work; one is convinced that it is not a character novel despite the persistent presence of a single central character, that it is not a portrayal of objective reality despite the vividly realistic scenes, that it is certainly not a novel of social protest. One notices that the central character simply drifts or is driven from place to place, meets different people, tries different jobs, different ways of life, and is at the end of the novel even less rooted in society than he was at the beginning. There is no obvious plot to the novel and no clear progression; there is little integration of characters or incidents; people simply appear and disappear; beasts disguised as people cheat, rob, assault, rape and kill; squalor succeeds squalor. And Manuel, generally impassive, drifts from scene to scene, apparently the sole thread. It is as though he were merely an excuse, a link between successive etchings of human degradation. Surely, one feels, there is something pathological about all this; the author is diseased, obsessed by his frightful Goyaesque vision of man's inhumanity to man. And then, suddenly, in a wholly unexpected context, one finds the author's own confession: 'En ese dolor sentido hay una satisfacción cruel, una voluptuosidad intensa.' Driven on by his obsession, it seems, — by his perverted puritanism, by his bitter disillusion with men, by the voluptuous fascination of suffering and squalor — the author has gone round the low quarter of Madrid, chatted to people, observed, taken notes, made sketches... and then invented Manuel as a means of bringing all this together into a single book. Little unity of plot; little character progression; little interaction of character and circumstances; simply a succession of Goyaesque etchings, with Manuel as the link between them.

But not the only link. Beyond Manuel — and beyond his principal co-plot-carrier, Roberto — we have seen pointers also to emotive unity: in the author's intense underlying subjectivity and in his consequently highly selective approach to real-life materials. Indeed, though it may seem strange to say this of such an apparent ragbag of 'apuntes del natural' ('un saco donde cabe todo', as the author believed a novel should be, VII, 1032), it could be argued that, beyond Manuel's presence as a mere linear link, the real unity of *La busca* — as of the trilogy of which it forms part — is largely poetic. Consideration of the third area of peculiarly Barojan emphasis, local colour, will take us a step closer to this view.

Baroja's emphasis on local-colour aspects of Madrid life was illustrated at length in the previous chapter and the evidence need not be repeated here. Like bestiality and extravagance, local colour is clearly seized upon by Baroja as an aspect of 'lo típico y lo característico', 'lo pintoresco y lo inmoral', 'la vida absurda, pero indudablemente [...] más divertida' of romantic Madrid; also, I suggest, as a further personal life-raft on which to seize amidst the 'corriente tumultuosa e inconsciente' of existence (VII, 598). Moreover, within the overall panorama of Baroja's areas of special emphasis, local colour can be seen as something of a bridge between the other two, with the picturesquely extravagant at one extreme (Don Alonso's 'Torre *Infiel*', El Tabuenca's 'rueda de barquillero', Tío Pérquique's cream cakes) and brutality at the other (the bullfight and La Blasa's tavern). In other words, no rigid separation is possible: one passes from extravagance and eccentricity to local colour and on to brutality, which in turn links up with the whole range of human degradation and associated living conditions.

Nevertheless, within this typically Barojan panorama there are notable differences of treatment. In particular, the central, local-colour range is commonly treated with irony; there is less irony in the author's treatment of extravagance and almost none in his treatment of brutality.

As my initial and principal example of ironic treatment I take an aspect of romantic Madrid that was intentionally omitted from the local-colour survey of the previous chapter: Doña Casiana's boarding-house. With its mingling of sordidness and frivolity, bullying and high spirits, it clearly lies in the intermediate range referred to above: with neither the extreme extravagance of the Rebolledos or the Aristas or Don Alonso, nor the extreme bestiality of El Bizco or the *golfos* or of living conditions in the Corralón. And the predominant tone is one of irony: irony about the house itself, 'la morada casta y pura de doña Casiana' (p. 258; a 1904 addition and a reminder, of course, of Faust's ecstatic aria, 'Salut, demeure chaste et pure', in Gounod's opera, elsewhere quoted by Baroja in its French original, II, 780), irony about Doña Casiana and her 'dulce sueño de burdel monstruo' (p. 259), about the paintings that adorned the walls and about the landlady's ambitions for them (p. 261; much developed in the 1904 version), about the 'régimen higiénico [de la casa] gracias [al cual] ninguno de los huéspedes caía enfermo de obesidad, de gota ni de cualquiera de esas otras enfermedades por exceso de alimentación, tan frecuentes en los ricos' (p. 264); irony, too, about the guests: about the 'señor viejo madrugador', for example, '[que] se entretenía tosiendo en la cama' (p. 258; a 1904 addition), about the three 'galantes damas' (p. 268; most commonly referred to directly in 1903 as 'las golfas') and about such aspects of their daily routine as the 'solemne ceremonia en la cual todas las mujeres de la casa salían al pasillo blandiendo el servicio de noche' (p. 270; cf. p. 262); irony, also, about the 'plácida sonrisa del alba' and the 'ejercicios musicales' of the cricket (p. 260; both absent in 1903); situational irony, too, in the juxtaposition of Irene's abortion and the celebrated arrival of a rich protector (p. 271) and in the juxtaposition of the sordid goings-on of the guests and the sentimental tunes played by the music box in the entrance hall (pp. 266, 271; both absent in 1903); irony, finally, in the author's attitude to his own efforts and limitations as a 'cronista imparcial y verídico' (most notably on pp. 257 and 260, with much 1904 addition and development). Moreover, this ironic tone continues in the opening pages of Part II, in the description of the *zapatería* (and again there is much 1904 addition and development). It disappears, however, during the Sunday meal in the Corralón (p. 283) as we come face to face with the first obvious beast in the novel, Vidal's mother, Leandra. Thereafter, except for situational irony to which we shall return, irony appears only sporadically, most notably in the description of the *tablao flamenco* (pp. 312-13).

How does one explain this notable disunity of tone in *La busca*, especially in view of my earlier suggestion that the unity of the work is perhaps largely poetic? The answer is necessarily hypothetical and subject to error. I suggest that Baroja starts his novel from a determined standpoint of ironic detachment, guided by the 'sentido un poco ácido y descarnado de los hechos pintorescos' that friends noted in him even during his student years (VII, 584), and that this is essentially a defensive mechanism, an early pointer to his subsequent quest for a state of '¡Ataraxia! ¡Serenidad!' (V, 366) — a state, incidentally, that has been much extolled, under the corresponding German word *Heiterkeit*, by another notable ironist, a contemporary of Baroja, Thomas Mann. So long as he is within an area of only limited evidence of human brutality or degradation — as in Doña Casiana's boarding-house and as in the *zapatería* — he can maintain that ironic standpoint. Faced, however, with more extreme evidence of degradation he becomes emotionally involved, his disgusted puritanism takes over, his defensive system breaks down and the tone ceases to be predominantly ironic. Moreover, the more deeply he finds himself immersed in the mire of debased humanity, the more desperately he needs to find a counterbalancing escape into eccentricity and extravagance. Thus, after his long initial immersion in degradation (Leandra and the Piratas, II,I; the Corralón, II,II;

the Corte de los Milagros, II,III; 'la vida en la zapatería', with a closing reminder of El Bizco's 'brutalidad y animalidad repelentes', II,IV) he finally feels the need for an escape into extravagance and thereafter oscillates between the one and the other: first, extravagance (the Rebolledos and the Aristas, II,IV), then degradation ('La taberna de la Blasa', II,V), then back to extravagance (Don Alonso and the story of his circus travels, II,VI). In the course of a less emotive local-colour chapter Baroja gradually finds again his standpoint of ironic detachment for the description of the *tablao flamenco* (II,VII), after which the oscillations succeed again with increasing violence: first the build-up to brutality that reaches a climax in Leandro's fight with El Valencia (II,VIII), then the most extravagant passage so far, Don Alonso's 'historia inverosímil' (II,IX), followed, in the same chapter, by the most bestial act so far, Leandro's killing of Milagros and himself (II,IX).

Of course, this is a manifestly oversimplified survey, for one finds oscillations also within individual chapters. In II,III, for example, one passes from the extravagance of Roberto's quest to the debased humanity of the beggars, back to Roberto's extravagance, on to the mingled humour and debasement of the *golfos*, on to further debasement, with a final return to Roberto's extravagance. The basic points, however, seem clear and indisputable: in the early part of the novel, both degradation and extravagance are present but they are reasonably contained and the tone is one of ironic detachment; when the evidence of degradation becomes greater, the ironic tone disappears, disgust (expressed both by characters and by the author) becomes more apparent and, as though to balance the increasing train of degradation, there is also, interwoven with it, an increasing train of extravagance. It may be that all this is merely a constructional device, a build-up of increasingly contrasting planes aimed at increasing vividness of effect. It is difficult, however, to accept that the disunity of tone is deliberate. My own feeling is that beneath the effective construction, very clearly, lies the personality of the author himself. The disunity of tone is itself a pointer to the essentially emotive unity of the work.

Further evidence of emotive unity is to be found in Baroja's use of situational irony. We have seen a notable example of such irony in the opening chapters of the novel: in the repeated juxtaposition of the sordid goings-on of the lodgers and the sentimental tunes played by the music box in the entrance hall. Whereas in verbal irony there is incongruity, for example, between the train of sordidness described in Doña Casiana's boarding-house and the author's reference to the house as a 'morada casta y pura', in situational irony the incongruity lies between the train of sordidness and a manifestly contrasting and strangely unintegrated element (in this case, the sentimentality represented by the music box). In both cases the reader is encouraged to see the train of sordidness as the reality; the comment, whether it be made directly by the narrator ('la morada casta y pura') or indirectly (here by the tunes of the music box, with the added indication by the author of the words of the tunes played), is seen as clearly discordant and inappropriate. Hence the humour. But such irony in Baroja produces not only humour; it produces also, often, a sense of pathos, an impression of disharmony between the world as it is and the world as it could be. Thus, Doña Casiana's boarding-house could be a 'morada casta y pura', but the evidence forces one to a very different view; one could live in an idealized world of zarzuelesque sentimentality (which gave Manuel 'la impresión de un mundo de placeres inasequible para él', pp. 269-70; almost certainly an autobiographical observation), but sordid goings-on convince one that it would be unrealistic. In other words, Baroja's irony commonly involves the contrasting juxtaposition of a sordid reality and an apparently unattainable ideal. It is a characteristic response, then, of someone like Baroja, 'realista con algo de romántico' (VII, 812): the romantic in him glimpses the illusion; the realist sees its futility. In the opening chapters of the novel, where human bestiality is limited in its range, the emphasis is on verbal irony; in the later chapters, where we are brought face to face with real human degradation, the narrator's verbal irony breaks down and the novelist's situational irony takes over.

There is an extremely effective example at the end of Part II of the novel. After increasing oscillation between bestiality and extravagance we proceed from the climax of extravagance (Don Alonso's most extravagant stories) to the climax of bestiality (Leandro's killing of Milagros and himself) and on to the final, characteristically Barojan scene of desolation.

> Durante toda la noche el señor Ignacio, sentado en una silla, lloró sin cesar; Vidal estaba asustado, y Manuel, también. La presencia de la muerte, vista tan de cerca, les aterrorizó a los dos.
>
> Y mientras lloraban dentro, en la calle las niñas cantaban a coro; y aquel contraste de angustia y de calma, de dolor y de serenidad, daba a Manuel una sensación confusa de la vida; algo pensaba él que debía de ser muy triste; algo muy incomprensible y extraño. (p. 324)[31]

On the one hand, the reality of suffering; on the other hand, the innocent, ingenuous unawareness of suffering. And the contrast produces, in the reader as in Manuel, 'una sensación confusa de la vida; algo [...] que debía de ser muy triste; algo muy incomprensible y extraño'. As the sense of contrast is now greater than in the example of the music box, so also the effect is more powerful. Basically, however, it is the same device and it produces a similar sense of anguish.

In the two examples of situational irony emphasized so far, the glimpsed plane of illusion is represented, first, by a music box (with the significant addition by the author of the words of the tune played), secondly, by young girls singing together in the street outside Ignacio's house. Far more commonly in *La busca*

31 The following recollection by Manso de Zúñiga of an incident many years later, when he was escorting Baroja round Vitoria and its surroundings, points to the peculiarly personal relevance and appeal to Baroja of the sort of contrast indicated above:

> Allí estuvimos paseando un rato, luego nos detuvimos en Escaño, donde los niños jugaban a canicas en la plaza. Don Pío le[s] preguntó si no había clase y el mayor respondió que "no porque la maestra echa sangre por la boca", respuesta que impresionó a don Pío y la anotó comentando lo terrible que era el contraste de aquellos niños jugando al sol y la pobre maestra tísica en la casa de al lado. (*12*, p. 51)

it is represented by nature, and I considered an example in Chapter 3 (above, pp. 35-7): at the end of a chapter of increasing evidence of sordidness and human degradation culminating in the marauding of El Bizco and his Piratas, Manuel 'se sentó a descansar un rato en el Campillo de Gil Imón' and there followed a description of the scene: notably detached from the world of human degradation previously described and with special emphasis, firstly on death and destruction (the cemetery and the sinister red sky) and, secondly, on nature's calm and serenity: in other words, both threatened retribution for so much degradation and a plane of illusion free from that degradation. Moreover, we noted that both these elements were much developed in the transition from the 1903 version to the 1904 version. Robert E. Lott has commented on the Campillo description as follows:

> Coincide el tono de la descripción con el estado afectivo de fastidio y disgusto de Manuel. Aquí, como en varios pasajes parecidos, la estrella y las montañas parecen simbolizar la pureza y paz remotas e inaccesibles. (*33*, p. 45)

These observations can perhaps be developed in two respects. In the first place, the description echoes not only Manuel's 'estado afectivo de fastidio y disgusto'; 'la pureza y paz remotas e inaccesibles', too, are relevant to the boy's state of mind, with his awareness of a 'mundo de placeres inasequible para él' (pp. 269-70). In the second place, the reader's standpoint is very close to Manuel's own, and Baroja's main concern, it seems, was less the relevance of the description to Manuel than the overall impact it would make on the reader. Here as elsewhere, Baroja writes not so much as a novelist concerned to probe character; far more as a poet concerned to arrive at a total integration of elements involving both characters and contexts and capable of communicating ultimately his own intensely personal response to life.[32]

One further example of situational irony must suffice. After

---

[32] I offer further evidence — and even proof — of this in 'The Pursuit of El Bizco: two versions', in a volume of studies presented to Professor Frank Pierce (Oxford: Dolphin, in press).

his experiences in Tío Patas' shop and the bakery and a brief
return to the boarding-house Manuel has again met El Bizco and
Vidal and there has been much emphasis on their exploitation of
others, on their callousness and on their *golfo* activities in
general. I start the quotation at the moment of transition to
other things:

> Escanció Vidal en las copas y bebieron los tres.
>
> Se veía Madrid en alto, con su caserío alargado y plano,
> sobre la arboleda del Canal. A la luz roja del sol poniente
> brillaban las ventanas con resplandor de brasa; destacábanse
> muy cerca debajo de San Francisco el Grande los rojos
> depósitos de la Fábrica del Gas, con sus altos soportes, entre
> escombreras negruzcas; del centro de la ciudad brotaban
> torrecillas de poca altura y chimeneas que vomitaban, en
> borbotones negros, columnas de humo inmovilizadas en el
> aire tranquilo. A un lado se erguía el Observatorio, sobre un
> cerrillo, centelleando el sol en sus ventanas; al otro, el
> Guadarrama azul, con sus crestas blancas, se recortaba en el
> cielo limpio y transparente, surcado por nubes rojas. (pp.
> 332-3)

One notes again the initial emphasis on the detachment of the
scene described ('*Se veía* Madrid *en alto*') and the subsequent
progression from the sordid world of man to the unsullied world
of nature. In the initial view of Madrid 'en alto' one recalls,
perhaps, Blanco Aguinaga's view of Madrid as a 'ciudadela a
conquistar'. But there is no apparent social or economic
implication; nor does the 'caserío' or the 'arboleda' suggest
oppression. Madrid, often — though not here — enveloped in
mist or dust in such panoramic descriptions, appears as a world
distant and detached, an appropriate image of that 'mundo de
placeres inasequible' that Manuel is vaguely aware of within
himself; an image, too, of that ideal world that seems constantly
to underlie Baroja's descriptions of debased humanity and to
explain the very darkness of his vision. Significantly, nature
again offers not only an image of purity (in the last sentence); it
also threatens the sordid world of man with destructive
retribution ('resplandor de brasa', 'nubes rojas'). All these

elements — sordidness, destructive threat and purity — were intensified in the 1903-4 revision.

To complement the above observations one can recall a revealing episode from *Aventuras, inventos y mixtificaciones de Silvestre Paradox*. It was referred to earlier, under 'Observation' (above, p. 58), for it points clearly to the initial conception of *La busca*, with visits to the low quarter and note-taking on what is observed there. Like Baroja himself, the protagonist is both fascinated and disgusted. We have seen the fascination. Now we must recall the disgust:

—¡Oh, la canalla miserable!

Y sentía que toda la podredumbre humana le rodeaba y acechaba. Si él hubiera sido tirano hubiese exterminado toda aquella morralla. Pero era sólo un pobre hombre, nada más. Después, para purificar su pensamiento con ideas más agradables, lo lanzaba al recuerdo de los grandes caminos solitarios, de los bosques de hayas y de encinas, de los montes perfumados por el aroma del tomillo. ¡Oh! ¡Quién le hubiera dado volar a los valles sombríos, a las playas desiertas!

Galeote triste de una vida miserable, remaba y remaba, azotado por la necesidad, sin objeto, sin fin, sin percibir a lo lejos la luz del faro, bajo un cielo negro, en un pantano turbio que reventaba en burbujas, producidas por exhalaciones de la porquería humana. (II, 110-11)

Disgust, thoughts of destruction, the evocation of untainted nature and the final realization that man, immersed in human degradation, can never attain the realm of purity of which nature is an image. The same elements underlie both *La busca* and the trilogy of which it forms part. In that, precisely, — and in the effectiveness with which those elements are communicated — lies the real unity of the work.

To illustrate this further I turn finally to the commonly stated view that *Aurora roja* gives sense and direction to the whole trilogy, and draw attention to the conclusion of each of the three volumes. In each case we find, juxtaposed, both disgust with humanity, culminating in notions of destruction, and the vision of a far better world, with nature as an image of that better world. We find also, at the end of the final volume, the ultimate realization that man can never attain the illusion that nature represents. In short: all the elements represented in the above passage from *Aventuras, inventos y mixtificaciones de Silvestre Paradox*.

Thus, in *La busca* Manuel's experiences culminate in notions of a revolt against society in which 'asesinaría a diestro y siniestro', 'ideas de exterminio' that subsequently give way to much thought as the 'bullicio febril de la noche' yields to 'la actividad serena y tranquila de la mañana'. Manuel finally reflects that he must be 'de los que trabajan al sol, no de los que buscan el placer en la sombra' (pp. 370, 373). The sun and the serenity of the morning — in contrast to the 'sombra' and the 'bullicio febril de la noche' — are clearly images of illusion. Similarly, at the end of *Mala hierba*, 'Manuel sentía una sorda irritación contra todo el mundo: un odio, hasta entonces amortiguado, se despertaba en su alma contra la sociedad, contra los hombres... [...]. Y, rabioso, invocó a todos los poderes destructores para que redujesen a cenizas esta sociedad miserable'. But 'el cielo estaba espléndido, cuajado de estrellas...' [the length of the passage inhibits adequate quotation]. 'No sé por qué hoy me consuela ver ese cielo tan hermoso', reflects Manuel to Jesús, and his friend talks 'con una voz serena de un sueño de humanidad idílica, un sueño dulce y piadoso, noble y pueril...':

> Una beatitud augusta resplandecía en el cielo, y la vaga sensación de la inmensidad del espacio, lo infinito de los mundos imponderables, llevaba a sus corazones una deliciosa calma.... (p. 507)

Finally, at the end of *Aurora roja*, after the held-out illusion of 'la aurora de un nuevo día, la aurora de la justicia [etc.]' and the contrasting reality of 'esta sociedad podrida' (*AR*, p. 630): 'Todos hablaron en el mismo sentido. Odio eterno, eterna execración contra la sociedad [...]. —¡Maldita vida!—murmuró [Manuel]—. Había que reducirlo todo a cenizas' (p. 644). Juan, the most idealistic of the anarchists, is buried and the novel concludes: 'Los obreros se cubrieron y en silencio fueron saliendo del camposanto. Luego, por grupos, volvieron por la carretera hacia Madrid. Había oscurecido' (p. 645). There is, after all, no dawn. With Juan's death illusion itself dies. The enticing vision of a better world that has been held out to us since the beginning of *La busca* has finally been banished and nature itself is in mourning. As a life story of Manuel the trilogy could indeed continue with further volumes, as countless commentators have pointed out. As an emotionally unified work it clearly finishes — and has to finish — at this point.

We can see now in what way *Aurora roja* gives sense and direction to the whole trilogy and it is clearly not in a real-life political sense. Indeed, as Puértolas and Moral have pointed out, in its emphasis on anarchism *Aurora roja* is the least objectively documented volume in the trilogy, for working-class political activity in Madrid was emphatically socialist rather than anarchist. But anarchism, both in its desperate desire to destroy 'esta sociedad podrida' and in its 'sueño de humanidad idílica', was the logical culmination of the duality of cruel reality and visionary idealism that runs through the whole trilogy. Indeed, at the end of *Mala hierba* — exactly parallel to the end of *La busca* — Juan tells Manuel for the first time, in the light of Manuel's destructive outburst, 'Eres un anarquista', and reveals that he too is an anarchist. '¿Desde cuándo?' asks Manuel. Jesús replies:

> —Desde que he visto las infamias que se cometen en el mundo; desde que he visto cómo se entrega fríamente a la muerte un pedazo de Humanidad; desde que he visto cómo mueren desamparados los hombres en las calles y en los hospitales. (*MH*, p. 507)

This is Baroja's own view exactly. He esteems Roberto for his realistic vision, but it is Jesús at this point and Juan throughout *Aurora roja* for whom he feels real affection, for the tempting anarchist dream of a new humanity is his own dream, too. Hence, throughout *La lucha por la vida*, amidst all the evidence of sordidness and human degradation, the repeated pointers to a contrasting plane of illusion. But amidst this duality of realism and romanticism that Baroja recognized within himself it is the implacable realism of his vision that predominates, darkened beyond mere reality by the author's very awareness of an ideal existence that men will never attain:

Ni los miserables se levantarán, ni resplandecerá un día nuevo, sino que persistirá la iniquidad por todas partes. Ni colectiva ni individualmente podrán libertarse los humildes de la miseria, ni de la fatiga, ni del trabajo constante y aniquilador. (*AR*, p. 643)

Hence the bitterness; hence the disillusion; hence the proclaimed futility of the anarchist dream ('noble y pueril', *MH*, p. 507; 'una bella ilusión', *AR*, p. 643). Hence too, finally, the desolate ending of *La lucha por la vida*.[33]

---

33 For the relevance of these findings to the '98 Generation in general, whose existence Baroja doubted and to which, in any case, he claimed he did not belong, see my article, 'The Spanish "Generation of 1898": II. A reinterpretation', *Bulletin of the John Rylands University Library of Manchester*, LVII (1974-5), 167-95 (especially 167-74, 189-95).

Bibliographical Note

BAROJA IN CONTEXT
1. Raymond Carr, *Spain 1808-1939*, Oxford, 1966. Includes a good survey of the period most relevant to *La lucha por la vida*, 1885-1902.
2. Donald L. Shaw, *The Generation of 1898 in Spain*, London and New York, 1975. Probably the best short introduction to the major figures of the '98 Generation.

BAROJA: GENERAL
3. Carmen Iglesias, *El pensamiento de Pío Baroja (Ideas centrales)*, México, 1963. Less concerned with mere thought and ideas than the title and subtitle suggest. Probably the best work on Baroja's basic view of life.
4. Biruté Ciplijauskaité, *Baroja, un estilo*, Madrid, 1972. The most revealing study so far on Baroja's novelistic art.
5. Beatrice Patt, *Pío Baroja*, Twayne's World Authors Series, 146, New York, 1971. A good general survey of Baroja's writings based on primary sources. Little specific on *La busca*.
6. Leo L. Barrow, *Negation in Baroja (A key to his novelistic creativity)*, Tucson, 1971. On the stylistic means by which Baroja creates the characteristic sense of desolation.
7. Carmen Iglesias, 'La controversia entre Baroja y Ortega acerca de la novela', *Hispanófila*, 1 (September 1959), 41-50. Reprinted in *13*. A good introduction to an important subject.
8. J. García Mercadal (ed.), *Baroja en el banquillo* (I. *Tribunal español*; II. *Tribunal extranjero*), Zaragoza [1947?]. A valuable collection of early critical material, much of it generally inaccessible.
9. *Indice (de Artes y Letras)*, 70-1 (January-February 1954). A good collection, with over forty contributions. Many of the best are republished in *10*. Good bibliography.
10. Fernando Baeza (ed.), *Baroja y su mundo*, 2 vols, Madrid, 1962. An excellent collection of studies: those in vol. I written expressly for the publication; those in vol. II republished from earlier sources. Good bibliography.
11. *Cuadernos Hispanoamericanos*, 265-7 (July-September 1972). An impressive centenary tribute with many good articles.
12. *Encuentros con don Pío (Homenaje a Baroja)*, Madrid, 1972. A centenary tribute with a few good contributions.
13. Javier Martínez Palacio (ed.), *Pío Baroja*, Madrid, 1974. A useful collection of previously published material, much of it from books and/or readily available elsewhere.

'*LA BUSCA*' IN CONTEXT

14. Andrenio (Eduardo Gómez de Baquero), *Novelas y novelistas*, Madrid, 1918.

15. Eugenio G. de Nora, *La novela española contemporánea*, I (1898-1927), Madrid, 1958.

16. Carlos Orlando Nallim, *El problema de la novela en Pío Baroja*, México, 1964.

17. Francisco J. Flores Arroyuelo, *Las primeras novelas de Pío Baroja (1900-1912)*, Murcia, 1967.

18. Emilio González López, *El arte narrativo de Pío Baroja (Las trilogías)*, New York, 1971.

19. Mary Lee Bretz, *La evolución novelística de Pío Baroja*, Madrid, 1979.

14-19 all have substantial sections on *La lucha por la vida*. *19* has the most up-to-date bibliography, but it needs supplementing, notably by that in *10*.

20. Soledad Puértolas, *El Madrid de 'La lucha por la vida'*, Madrid, 1971. Extensive background quotation from the press of the Regency period (1885-1902).

21. Carmen del Moral Ruiz, *La sociedad madrileña fin de siglo y Baroja*, Madrid, 1974. Impressive documentation on economic and social conditions in the poor quarters of Madrid.

22. Luis Maristany, 'La concepción barojiana de la figura del golfo', *Bulletin of Hispanic Studies*, XLV (1968), 102-22. Good documentation on Baroja and on contemporary studies of the *golfo*.

23. Olga Kattan, 'Madrid en *Fortunata y Jacinta* y en *La lucha por la vida*: dos posturas', in *Cuadernos Hispanoamericanos*, 250-2 (October 1970-January 1971), 546-78. Surveys the documentary aspects of Baroja's work.

24. Pablo Beltrán de Heredia, 'Regeneracionismo noventayochista en *La lucha por la vida*' [1972], in *13*, pp. 149-64. Finds disillusioned *regeneracionismo* and an Institution-influenced concern with restoration and salvation.

25. Hans Jörg Neuschäfer, 'Apuntes para una historia social del naturalismo español: la imagen del pueblo desde Galdós hasta Blasco Ibáñez', *Iberoromania*, new series, 7 (1978), 28-34. Questionable presentation of Manuel as the epitome of the *cuarto estado* and its aspirations.

26. Antonio Risco, '*La lucha por la vida* de Baroja en la evolución de la novelística española', *Revista Canadiense de Estudios Hispánicos*, II (1977-8), 258-81. Considers the trilogy's relationship to the picaresque novel.

LA BUSCA

27. Joaquín de Entrambasaguas, *Las mejores novelas contemporáneas*, II, Barcelona, 1958, pp. 1323-44. A useful general survey.

28. Gonzalo Torrente Ballester, '*La lucha por la vida*', in *10*, I, pp. 125-37. A perceptive study of Baroja's narrative technique with emphasis on the linear linking of 'apuntes del natural'.

29. Carlos Blanco Aguinaga, *Juventud del 98*, Madrid, 1970, pp. 229-90 ('Realismo y deformación escéptica: la lucha por la vida según don Pío

Baroja'). Probably the most influential and most misleading of recent studies on Baroja. Discussed at length in Chapter 6.

30. D. Howitt, 'Baroja's Preoccupation with Clocks and his Emphatic Treatment of Time in the Introduction to *La busca*', in *Hispanic Studies in Honour of Joseph Manson*, Oxford, 1972, pp. 139-47. Points to relevant sound imagery in *La busca*, I,i.

31. Javier Martínez Palacio, 'Baroja y un personaje de acción: Roberto Hasting', *Insula*, 308-9 (July-August 1972), 10. Contains a number of hypotheses that *La busca* 1903 shows to be mistaken.

32. Javier Martínez Palacio, 'La creación del espacio en *La lucha por la vida*', *Sin Nombre*, II, 4 (1972), 33-8. Finds imagery of labyrinth, hell and cemetery, allegedly relevant to Blanco Aguinaga's notion of exploitation.

33. Roberto E. Lott, 'El arte descriptivo de Pío Baroja', in *11*, pp. 26-54 (especially pp. 44-53: '*La lucha por la vida*: descripciones del paisaje y del medio ambiente y sus contextos y funciones'). Emphasizes the functional relevance of descriptions.

34. Alfonso Rey Alvarez, 'La originalidad de *La busca*', *Revista de Letras* (Puerto Rico), XV (1972), 423-33. Emphasizes Baroja's 'descripciones de ambientes', in contrast to the psychological probing of Galdós and Alas.

35. Rogelio Reyes Cano, 'Sobre la técnica descriptiva de *La busca*, de Baroja', *Archivo Hispalense*, LVI (1973) [vol. II], 167-84. Finds significant selection and literary technique in Baroja's descriptions; serves nicely to complement *33*.

36. Emilio Alarcos Llorach, *Anatomía de 'La lucha por la vida'*, Madrid, 1973. The most substantial study published so far; a valuable complement to my own present study, with rather different emphasis and findings.

37. Ricardo Senabre, 'Notas sobre la elaboración de *La busca*', *Archivum*, XXVI (1976), 391-401. Considers aspects of the 1903-4 revision.

38. Antonio Risco, 'Estructura de una novela picaresca de Baroja, *La busca*', in Manuel Criado de Val (ed.), *La picaresca: orígenes, textos y estructuras*, Madrid, 1979, pp. 865-76. A more readable and more *La busca*-oriented version of *26*.

39. María Embeita, '*La lucha por la vida*', in *La picaresca* (see *38*), pp. 877-92. Examines Manuel's development, with emphasis on the emotive and moral relevance of accompanying physical descriptions.

40. H. Ramsden, *Pío Baroja: 'La busca' 1903 to 'La busca' 1904*, Durham Modern Languages Series, Durham, 1982. Surveys the main aspects of the 1903-4 revision and finds confirmation of points made in the present study.